GUNAHOLIC

WHY I NO LONGER CARRY

BY CHIP PLUNKETT

RETIRED NYC POLICE OFFICER AND GUN CONTROL ADVOCATE

GUNAHOLIC

Copyright © 2023 by Chip Plunkett

All Rights Reserved

No part of this publication may be reproduced, distributed, or transmitted in any form or by any means, including photocopying, recording, or other electronic or mechanical methods, or by any information storage and retrieval system without the prior written permission of the author and publisher, except in the case of very brief quotations embodied in critical reviews and specific other noncommercial uses permitted by copyright law.

Educators may enjoy legal copyright exemptions to facilitate their teaching and classroom lessons. Thank you for your services.

WHY I NO LONGER CARRY

Cover Photo:

The author's patrol car after an armed chase and collision. The author's partner was killed (RIP); The author was also pronounced dead on arrival but was revived. YouTube Video: Police Chase Aftermath - Bronx, June 1988

Note to reader:

Specific details are reiterated throughout the bullet points (chapters), so you can read them in any order. Due to the topic's sensitivity, please do not quote individual sentences out of context. Quoting out of context can portray an entirely different meaning.

Thank you.

GUNAHOLIC

WHY I NO LONGER CARRY

TABLE OF CONTENTS

DEDICATION

BRIEF INTRODUCTION

WHY I AM WRITING THIS BOOK

BULLET POINT 1
IS GUN ADDICTION REAL?

BULLET POINT 2
WHAT IF YOU DON'T KNOW GUNS?

GUNAHOLIC

BULLET POINT 3

DO GUN LAWS HELP?

BULLET POINT 4

DO SAFES & MAG LIMITS HELP?

BULLET POINT 5

SHOULD WE BAN ASSAULT RIFLES?

BULLET POINT 6

ARE GUN RIGHTS UNLIMITED?

BULLET POINT 7

DO GUNS AFFECT THE BORDER?

BULLET POINT 8

SECOND AMENDMENT & TYRANNY

WHY I NO LONGER CARRY

BULLET POINT 9

ARE GUNS A "GOD-GIVEN" RIGHT?

BULLET POINT 10

DOES RESEARCH SUPPORT GUNS?

BULLET POINT 11

DO MORE GUNS = LESS CRIME?

BULLET POINT 12

ARE LAWS UNFAIR TO GUN OWNERS?

BULLET POINT 13

WHAT AGENCY REGULATES GUNS?

BULLET POINT 14

IS IT OKAY TO KEEP GUNS HOME?

BULLET POINT 15

IS MOST CRIME BLACK-ON-BLACK?

GUNAHOLIC

BULLET POINT 16

ARE THERE REASONS TO CARRY?

BULLET POINT 17

ARE GUNS THE CORE PROBLEM?

BULLET POINT 18

ACTION PLAN

POSTSCRIPT

ABOUT THE AUTHOR

& FINAL THOUGHTS

WORKS CITED

WHY I NO LONGER CARRY

DEDICATION

This book is dedicated to all victims of gun violence, their families, local communities, and the first responders and medical professionals involved.

I want to take this opportunity to acknowledge Gary Peaco and his family. Gary was my partner in the New York City Housing Police Department (now the Housing Bureau of the NYPD). Gary also served as a pastor at a church in Central Harlem, where he was sorely missed. He died due to gun violence in the South Bronx in 1988. Though he did not die from gunshot wounds, the guns fired from the back window of the stolen police car we were chasing caused our collision and his murder (see cover photo). Gary left behind a loving wife and their then 3-year-old twin daughters. May he rest in peace.

GUNAHOLIC

WHY I NO LONGER CARRY

BRIEF INTRODUCTION

Thank you for considering this book. I have owned guns since childhood and am a survivor of gun violence. I feel I was addicted to guns – a gunaholic. I am very familiar with guns, especially handguns, and (for what it is worth) was one of the top shooters at the public and police firing ranges I frequented for years.

I have heard many arguments from both pro-gun and anti-gun advocates. All have flaws and biases. I will simplify them in case you are not very familiar with guns. However, I will not dumb this down for you or anyone. It is too important of a topic.

GUNAHOLIC

The Bottom line is that we need total, comprehensive, and multi-faceted gun control. I hope to prove to you why our current piecemeal efforts at gun control are like giving pacifiers to crying babies and not solving our thirst for real change regarding gun violence.

WHY I NO LONGER CARRY

WHY I AM WRITING THIS BOOK

To Share an Inside Scoop on Gun Control

Dear Reader,

Before slavery was abolished, Abraham Lincoln proposed its "gradual emancipation" to appease slave owners (Library of Congress, 2023). Today, like Lincoln, well-intentioned Americans offer diluted gun laws to (sometimes) appease gun owners. Though Lincoln "personally abhorred slavery" (Library of Congress, 2021), it took a Civil War to attain his goal.

America lost more lives to gun violence than the Civil War and all wars combined (Bailey, 2017). On average, we lose over one hundred Americans to gun violence daily. That's out of more than three hundred people shot every day (Gramlich, 2023) (Hemenway & Miller, 2000). We must unshackle ourselves from the gun lobby and no longer settle for 'gradual emancipation' from gun violence. Only then can we achieve our inalienable rights of "life, liberty, and the pursuit of happiness" (US 1776).

If you think our mishmash of gun laws works, please take some time to speak with a few victims of gun violence. Or read some of their stories, such as (Hogg, 2018) (Parker A, 2019) (Schumann, 2021) and numerous others. (I am not assuming that you have not.)

Both sides of the gun debate promote legislation that makes gun violence worse. By 'sides,' I realize you may fall somewhere on one or both sides or have distinct views. Please pardon this and a few other word choices. I also intentionally repeat some points so you can read chapters out of order. I am not a professional writer – I'm just a grandfather, a business owner, and an injured and retired police officer. Nevertheless, I will do my best to share little-known insights outside of gun culture and, in some regards, outside of law enforcement.

Gun rights advocates sometimes lack patience with those who want more gun control. They assume they're unpatriotic or naïve. On the flip side, many gun control advocates assume all gun owners are extremists. They are unfamiliar with the nuances of the legislation they promote because they are on the outside of gun culture, looking in and not fully understanding.

I am familiar with both sides of the debate because I live in both worlds. I know firearms and the gun culture intimately. However, I have since come to believe in complete and multi-faceted gun control. By that, I mean 'gun reform.' Only comprehensive and multi-faceted gun regulations have evidence-based support for making substantial changes in our epidemic of gun violence (Duchesne J, 2022) (Kalesan, 2016) (Kwon, 2005). Our feel-good gun control legislation mostly proves impotent and more fatal.

I have relevant and timely information to share with you – the concerned reader. I am not the only one with this inside info, but I am in an excellent position to share it. I have owned guns my entire life, including a family gun passed along in trust at birth.

The first gun I purchased as a young teen was an illegal firearm, a fact I quickly learned. My dad thought it was funny that I bought a sawed-off shotgun from Sonny, an elderly gangster living down the block. He proudly told that story to his buddies for years. Nevertheless, he returned it, got my newspaper route money back, and told Sonny never to look at me again. He did not.

I concealed-carried handguns most of my adult life, including in high-crime neighborhoods as a cop and a civilian. I am a gun violence survivor. I was seriously injured, presumed dead, and retired early from the police department. My noble partner was killed. Though I am probably the oldest on the team, I still volunteer on a police support task force that responds to NYPD shootings and suicides. These life experiences and others inform my views on gun violence. I will probably write things you agree with and others you will not. Hopefully, you will still find helpful information regardless of personal opinions.

WHY I NO LONGER CARRY

I have a concealed carry license in New York and am authorized to carry pistols nationally. Nevertheless, I chose not to carry as I did for years. There was just too much gun violence for me to rationalize being part of this gun culture any longer. Statistically, and based on my health, I probably don't have much time left. However, too much misrepresenting facts on both sides of our gun debate costs lives. I, therefore, feel compelled to help clear away some of the more critical misunderstandings.

For example, gun rights advocates often say guns cannot be limited. However, gun ownership always had limits – before and well after the Second Amendment (Austin, 2013) (Cornell, 2008) (Smyth, 2020) (Spitzer, 2017) (U.S. Supreme Court, 2008) (Waldman, 2015) (Winkler, 2011).

On the other side of the debate, gun control advocates promote mental health safeguards, firearm safe storage mandates, and magazine ('mag') capacity limits. None of this tilts the scales:

Most shooters are not linked with mental illness (Brucato, 2021) (McGraw, 2021); Many gun owners keep at least one accessible loaded gun at home even if all their other firearms are stored in a safe (Hoskins K, 2020); Magazine restrictions do not work as much as we would like either – most victims are shot with just one or two bullets from standard capacity pistols, and not assault rifles with high-capacity mags (Braga AA, 2018) (FBI, Expanded Homicide Data Table 8, 2019).

(Note: Some define assault rifles as fully automatic. I will use the more commonly understood definition and elaborate later.)

On a personal note, I used to keep a tiny pocket pistol on me in the confines of our home. I would keep a much larger gun by my bedside at night. I wouldn't go anywhere without a firearm, not even to put out the trash. This type of vigilance (some say paranoia) is common among gun owners, particularly those carrying for self-defense. The catchphrase in the gun culture is, "I'd rather have a gun and not need one than need one and not have it." You always carry "just in case" you need the gun.

It does not matter what a gun looks like or how many rounds ('bullets') it holds. All guns kill. We must drastically reduce the number of firearms and limit them to those with a proven need for a deadly weapon. If limitations to the Second Amendment sound unconstitutional, they are not (District of Columbia v. Heller, 2008). There is an entire section on that later.

America repeatedly achieved what we thought was impossible. Americans have another golden opportunity to live up to our Constitution's preamble to "promote the general Welfare, and secure the Blessings of Liberty to ourselves and our Posterity" (U.S. Const. pmbl.).

I thank you for considering this book and hope you continue reading. I trust you will learn something valuable, but please pardon my unsophisticated writing and dated vocabulary.

GUNAHOLIC

BULLET POINT 1

IS GUN ADDICTION REAL?

Yes, And I'm a Recovering Gunaholic

Many have heard about links between school shooters and bullying. Some high-profile school shooters had a history of being bullied or mistreated. They suffered anxiety, depression, and similar conditions (Dowdell, 2022) (Dutton, 2013).

These school shooters found temporary relief as they obsessed with guns (Dutton, 2013) (Rosenthal, 2019). This addictive behavior is familiar to those with other addictions, such as drugs, alcohol, sex, and gambling (Martinez, 2018) (Yücel, 2019). Such behavior helps one temporarily escape feelings of insecurity, inadequacy, and social isolation (Kimmel, 2020).

Researchers say guns also help some feel like they are more masculine (Borgogna, 2022) (Chang, 2018). A casual review of firearms product catalogs, websites, and advertising reveals that the gun industry caters to male insecurity and masculinity (Posess, 2020).

This does not imply that if someone carries a gun, there is a history of bullying or feelings of inadequacy. Generalizations are divisive, and that would be another stereotype. Since guns are integral to American culture, all demographics and personality types own and carry firearms. On the other hand, you do not have to be a school shooter or insecure male to obsess with guns.

Nevertheless, the more one tries to escape from memories of bullying, childhood trauma, insecurity, lack of confidence, manhood issues, etc., the more alluring guns can be (Borgogna, 2022) (Chang, 2018) (Posess, 2020). Like other addictions, gun addiction also leads to problems with money and relationships. As it consumes one's life, it leads to denial and lying to self and others. Excuses for obsessive behaviors related to firearms become more frequent.

Those more obsessed will constantly search for the best gun to carry or the most potent bullet to load their favorite pistol with. They compare firearm specifications and bullet ballistics charts until their eyes are blurry. They substitute family activities with time at the range. They fixate on having the perfect gun that will never malfunction (note: it does not exist) and carry a second gun, or even a third, "just in case" the other guns malfunction.

The more extreme of these personality types cannot live without guns (Powell, 2016). The more they focus on guns, the more they dwell on the mostly imaginary possibility of needing one for self-defense. Eventually, they lose their self-confidence to defend themselves without a gun (Chang, 2018).

They carry a gun inside their well-alarmed homes in low-crime neighborhoods. They do not go anywhere without a weapon. They justify this excessive attachment to firearms by convincing themselves that they may one day need a gun to protect themselves or others (Garfinkel, 2018) (Martinez, 2018).

Gun addiction leads to excessive purchases of firearms and ammunition ('ammo') to help feel better. As drug addicts congregate with other drug users, gunaholics surround themselves with other gun owners. Their friends and activities change as loved ones look on and try to understand the deeper issues they may be masking. Addiction research shows that the same brain chemical released with other addictions, including drugs, gambling, and sex – dopamine – is released with gun addiction (Garfinkel, 2018).

In full disclosure, I recently had to transport one of my pistols after not carrying it for some time. Like an alcoholic who just sipped a drink after abstaining, that almost pulled me back into daily carry. It was tough to put my pistol back in the gun safe. Guns are like powerful drugs. I understand addiction, and I am certainly addicted to guns. As they say at AA or other twelve-step meetings: "Hello, my name is Chip, and I am a gunaholic." For much of the above, I could just as easily have been talking about my own behaviors.

I once confiscated crack cocaine from an addict who was street-dealing. She accidentally dropped some of the cocaine on the dirty sidewalk. I will never forget how fast she dodged down to save as much cocaine as possible from within crevices in the concrete.

The same knee-jerk reaction can be seen when gun addicts hear about gun control, particularly after a mass shooting. The gunaholic feels life cannot be lived without firearms. And as I just admitted, I am speaking from experience and not righteously pointing fingers.

GUNAHOLIC

BULLET POINT 2

WHAT IF YOU DON'T KNOW GUNS?

That's Not Important ~ Just Know 'All' Guns Kill

Don't worry if you do not know the difference between a pistol and a revolver, or an automatic and semiautomatic. Firearms shoot bullets, bullets kill, and therefore all guns kill. This is the crucial thing to focus on.

Gun rights advocates often mock those discussing gun control for not knowing about firearms. However, you don't have to know anything about guns to promote their control. Guns kill – the rest is the small print. It does not matter what a gun looks like or how many bullets it holds. Some firearms should be immediately banned, especially for civilians, but all guns are lethal.

I will limit this simplified explanation to common semiautomatic pistols and assault rifles (AR15s). This is to help you better understand their basics. But let me stress that you do not have to know firearms to know they 'all' kill. (As mentioned, I am using the common definition of assault rifles for now.)

Let us briefly start with bullets. A "bullet" is technically just that lead projectile ejected from the tip of a bullet "cartridge" or "round." It is not that entire piece of ammunition as many (including some gun owners) assume. After pulling the trigger, gunpowder explodes, and the lead "bullet" ejects.

For simplicity, I will primarily refer to bullets, cartridges, and rounds using the single colloquial term "bullet." I will also use some other shooting vernacular. Please excuse the simplifications. This is not a gun parts manual – it is informative but not needlessly technical.

Whether you are shooting a pistol or an assault rifle, when you pull the trigger, a bullet fires. Then, the mechanics of the firearm automatically feeds ('loads') the next bullet for you to shoot. All you need to do is pull the trigger again. That is what "semiautomatic" means. There are no hammers to cock or bolts to slide to get the next bullet ready. The firearm did all the required steps. All that is needed for the next shot is for you to pull the trigger again … and again …

(Fully automatic machine guns are the same, except the bullets keep firing until you stop pressing the trigger.)

Most pistols and assault rifles are semiautomatic and use magazines that conveniently hold the bullets. After a magazine with, for example, ten bullets is finished, you eject that magazine and insert a new one. You then pull the trigger again ten times for another ten shots… and change that now-used magazine with another fully loaded magazine ... ad infinitum.

That takes only 1 to 2 seconds for most shooters to eject an empty mag and insert a new one preloaded with another 10 (more or less) bullets. Don't worry about how magazines are replaced –know it is quick and easy.

Semiautomatics are particularly lethal because one shooter can keep reloading the same gun with new mags and quickly kill or injure thousands if not stopped. If a shooter has fifty spare mags, it's like carrying fifty guns. Some refer to semiautomatic pistols and rifles as "weapons of mass destruction." One teenager with a common semiautomatic can fire more bullets ('rounds per minute') than 15 Revolutionary War soldiers. If that teenager adds a simple bump stock, it will fire more rounds than 250 soldiers (Schildkraut, 2019) (Weapons of War, 2023) (Military, 2023). Today's assault rifle bullets are also exponentially more lethal and travel at around 3X the speed of sound.

As of this writing, the most casualties (shot, injured, or killed) from "one person" with assault rifles and multiple mags was an estimated 867. Thousands, if not millions more, were affected by that atrocity in Las Vegas in 2017. One deranged monster fired over one thousand bullets in only ten minutes. I will not mention the shooter's name out of respect for the victims and their families (Statista, 2023) (Trotta, 2017).

It makes sense that our police are better armed than the public – unless you fear the government. 'Government' includes police and other law enforcement for extreme Second Amendment fundamentalists. Encounters have been fatal. They commonly say, "I am my police department." The extreme-right media is especially critical of the ATF, the Department of Justice, and the FBI.

Many with this distrust of our government believe they should be equally or better armed in case of government tyranny (Cooter, 2022) (Pason, 2021). Such fear is often based on misinterpretations of the Second Amendment and the US Constitution (ibid.). As mentioned, there is an important chapter devoted to that later.

For now, police and most civilians who carry pistols typically carry more than one magazine. Police are often outgunned since they have more restrictions on firearms than the public (Mustard, 2000). Police casualties are increasingly the result of assault rifles with high-capacity magazines. However, most police are killed with pistols (Crifasi CK, 2016) (ODMP, 2023). Moreover, more police are killed in States with less restrictive gun laws (Homeland Security, 2021) (ODMP, 2023) (Swedler DI, 2015).

Assault rifles (and other rifles) are generally shot more accurately than pistols since they are longer and thus easier to aim. Nevertheless, pistols can fire the same number of bullets as rifles since both are easily reloaded with easy-to-insert magazines. So please do not limit your gun control efforts to assault rifles. Standard capacity pistols are just as dangerous in the real world and kill more people, even if you include all mass shootings (Braga AA, 2018) (FBI, Expanded Homicide Data Table 8, 2019).

Pistols and assault rifles are available as "fully" automatic if you have the credentials. However, semiautomatics can also be fired rapidly. They are so lethal that most standard-issue military assault rifles are, in fact, "semiautomatic" like the civilian versions. Military assault rifles are 'not' all fully automatic machine guns (Military.com, 2023) as some gun rights advocates claim. Only some are, not all. That is a common deceptive tactic to portray civilian models as less lethal than military versions.

Civilians are armed with assault rifles designed for combat with no substantial differences from standard-issue military assault rifles (Military.com, 2023). Do not let anyone tell you otherwise. The differences are insignificant.

There are endless sizes, shapes, and types of firearms. Whether assault rifles or tiny pocket pistols, they all shoot bullets, and all bullets kill. As such, all guns must be strictly regulated to reduce gun violence. Everything else is the fine print and a fatal delay.

GUNAHOLIC

BULLET POINT 3

DO GUN LAWS HELP?

Some, But Many Delay Reform

Do you wonder why horrific mass shootings cannot get us to enact gun reform? Much has to do with the voting style of gun rights advocates. They often vote for nothing but the absolute elimination of regulations. In comparison, gun control advocates typically vote on various issues and may not put gun control at the top. Even if a majority of Americans want gun control, the laser-focused gun-rights bloc casts more votes against it (Joslyn, 2017) (Lacombe, 2021) (Tatalovich, 2022).

Politicians on both sides know this. Regardless of the party in power, they all appease the gun lobby. It's been this way for years and across many administrations. The difference is mostly words, not actions. Many like to blame the other party. That is counterproductive and keeps us divided on this and other issues.

The gun industry benefits from our mishmash of laws that keep Americans unfocused on gun reform. Gun sales spike after high-profile mass shootings when gun owners fear additional restrictions (Busse, 2021) (Powell J L, 2020). These gun laws give false hope – and delay what is required – comprehensive gun control (Diaz, 2013) (Duchesne J, 2022) (Kalesan, 2016) (Kwon, 2005). Despite many gun laws, guns sell at a significant cost to life and liberty.

Let's say you go to a pharmacy, but they cannot legally sell you because you don't have a prescription. "Don't worry," the clerk tells you, "Our friends around the corner aren't licensed and can legally sell you without a prescription." They may even call them for you.

That's how the gun show loophole works. Federal law requires only "licensed" dealers to do background checks. However, their unlicensed friends can legally sell you without background checks. There are more details, but that's the essence of the "gun show loophole." It is not limited to gun shows, but since unlicensed dealers frequent gun shows, the term "gun show loophole" stuck. You can legally purchase firearms from various unlicensed sellers that have nothing to do with gun shows, and you can even buy guns online in many States. Nevertheless, there are about 4,000 gun shows annually (Giffords, 2023). If you have time, search for gun shows near you.

When my friends and I were just below the legal age to buy beer, we would ask older friends to buy it. That's what a straw purchase of firearms is. You get someone else to buy the gun because you cannot legally purchase firearms. Underage teens from NJ crossed into our neighborhood in NY to buy alcohol because our drinking age was lower. It is the same with guns. People buy guns in States or cities where it's easier to purchase them.

If a carload of underage teens drink at a bar and die in an auto wreck, the bar gets sued. What if the same underage teens bought guns and killed someone? Would the gun manufacturer or dealer get sued? No. By law, they are largely exempt from liability (Congress.gov, 2005) (Giffords, 2023) (Hals, 2022).

You cannot drink and drive. However, several States have no prohibitions about drinking and carrying firearms. You can go to shooting ranges with your assault rifles and cases of beer and fire away. Alternatively, you can drink at the local bar while carrying your guns.

If you drive after drinking and crash, you can be arrested for drunk driving but not for carrying a lethal weapon while intoxicated. Not all States have laws that prohibit being intoxicated when carrying a firearm (Carr, 2010) (USCCA, 2019).

In Texas, if you leave your loaded gun accessible to a child in the house, you are legally liable. But not if you work in an "agricultural enterprise." If you're working in agriculture, you are exempt! This and other examples above demonstrate the flaws of our gun laws. (Texas Statutes, 2023).

Our elected officials enact laws that barely impact gun violence. They sometimes are praised by the media for passing bipartisan gun legislation. Regardless, until our elected representatives 'comprehensively' regulate firearms like we do prescription drugs, and until we strictly limit gun licenses and require liability insurance as we do with automobiles, we will keep watching the same horrific news.

This book is a wake-up call for some and will anger others. Our gun laws do not work – we need to regulate all guns and drastically limit who gets to carry them in public. The more fragmented gun laws we have, the more false hope we cling to, and the further we are from effective gun reform (Duchesne J, 2022) (Kalesan, 2016) (Kwon, 2005).

The main reason we may ever need a gun is to protect us from … guns. Think about that.

GUNAHOLIC

WHY I NO LONGER CARRY

BULLET POINT 4

DO SAFES & MAG LIMITS HELP?

Yes, But They Also Delay Gun Reform

Storing guns in safes is like parking cars in garages. Garages do not prevent speeding.

Limiting magazines to 10 bullets (rounds) is like giving ten bats to a gangster. Ten-round mags do not prevent murder.

It is crucial to regulate 'all' firearms to reduce gun violence. Limited gun legislation takes the focus away from comprehensive regulations, and we lose even more lives (Duchesne J, 2022) (Kalesan, 2016) (Kwon, 2005). We get steamrolled by the gun industry, which couldn't care less about gun safes and magazine capacity (Busse, 2021) (Powell J L, 2020).

I know many gun owners, and I don't think any of them keep all their guns in a safe. I didn't. Like most who carry guns, I was ready for the unlikely worst-case scenario. You always keep at least one fully loaded gun on or near you, not in the safe. Regarding magazine capacity, remember that handguns kill more people in America than all assault rifles with high-capacity magazines combined (ATF, 2023) (FBI, Expanded Homicide Data Table 8, 2019).

Gun safes are one of those feel-good topics that gun control advocates focus on. I admire their zeal, and yes, gun safes prevent some deaths. And that is significant. However, the loaded guns kept outside the safe are the problem, not the unused guns that collect dust in a safe.

Gun control advocates often reference a 2016 survey of only a few gun owners (Cassandra K. Crifasi, 2018). It had a high nonresponse rate, so the researchers gave gift cards to entice participation. Its focus group consisted of just sixteen firearms owners from Texas gun clubs (many of whom knew each other). The survey asked, "Do you secure your gun with a trigger lock 'or other lock?'" That's a confusing survey question – I will explain why:

The researchers knew little about firearms. I am not faulting them for that. However, they didn't know that "or other lock" can be confused with "locked and loaded." In gun lingo, "Locked and loaded" is NOT locked. It means your pistol (1911 or another single-action style) is loaded, and its thumb 'safety' is switched on to help prevent unintentional discharges. That means the thumb safety helps the owner avoid accidentally shooting it, but it's not a "lock." Many unfortunate children quickly switched that nominal 'lock' off before killing themselves. Moreover, most pistols sold do not have a thumb or manual trigger safety.

Some gun owners in that survey surely counted their easy-to-move thumb safety as "or other lock." However, that's hardly the same as storing their pistol in a safe. Many gun control advocates are not very knowledgeable about gun culture. You do not have to know gun parts to promote gun control. However, when promoting certain legislation, a basic understanding will help.

Many gun owners store their unused guns in a safe, primarily so they are not 'stolen.' That's gun security – not safety. Family members are commonly shown how to open the safe if they need a gun in an emergency. Unfortunately, family members are killed with firearms owned by other family members many times more than they are used to shoot home invaders (Kellermann AL, 1998) (Lee LK, 2022).

To repeat, many keep their day-to-day firearm(s) fully loaded and accessible – and not in a safe (Salhi C, 2021). "Why keep my gun in a safe if I may need it to protect my family?" they rhetorically ask. Politicians can legislate all they want about gun safes, but it will not prevent most gun deaths.

Magazine capacity limits can also help, but that has limited effect and delays authentic gun reform. All magazines should be strictly limited. Gun control advocates often reference an academic study that reviews just sixty-nine "high fatality" mass shootings (Klarevas, 2019). It compares high-capacity mags to regular mags used in these shootings.

Without going into unnecessary methodology, they use the "mean" instead of the "median" average and change the definition of "mass shooting" from the commonly accepted one. That allows them to exaggerate the number of deaths from high-capacity magazines.

You do not have to know statistics to understand that the more bullets, the more deaths. However, it only takes one or two shots for most to die. This statistical sloppiness makes us think regular capacity magazines are significantly less lethal. Regular-capacity firearms kill more people. All guns are lethal regardless of whether they have ten bullet mags (standard-capacity) or 11+ bullet mags (high-capacity) (Smyth, 2020).

GUNAHOLIC

What if a shooter has one 15-round high-capacity mag? And another shooter has three 10-round standard cap mags. Who has more bullets to kill with? The shooter with standard cap magazines has double the bullets. Magazines are changed in just seconds. You can regulate magazine capacity all you want, but it is primarily ineffective unless you restrict all magazines. Magazines are for combat, not self-defense.

Studies like the one referenced above indirectly serve to delay comprehensive gun control. Do not settle for gun safes and low-capacity magazines from your elected officials – demand absolute gun control. Everything else is a chimera and delays our emancipation from gun violence.

BULLET POINT 5

SHOULD WE BAN ASSAULT RIFLES?

Yes, But Handguns Kill More

(As mentioned, some comments are repeated so you can read bullet points out of order. This chapter has several repeats because of the popularity of the subject. 'Assault rifle' and 'AR15' are used interchangeably. I use the more common definition of 'assault rifle' unless specified.)

You do not have to know much about guns. Any firearm, large or small, high-capacity magazine or standard capacity, fires bullets. Guns don't kill; bullets do. That is the critical point. All firearms must be regulated if we desire the right to life and liberty for all (Diaz, 2013). Assault rifles are lethal, but many more Americans are killed with handguns (ATF, 2023) (FBI, Expanded Homicide Data Table 8, 2019) (Smyth, 2020).

There's a plethora of misinformation about assault rifles. Many gun rights advocates erroneously say civilian assault rifles differ vastly from military assault rifles. That's misleading. Assault rifles were designed for military combat (assault), and there is very little difference between the civilian version and the 'standard issue' military version.

The standard issue military version is not typically a "fully automatic machine gun." NRA representatives repeat that myth in defense of civilian assault rifles and try to rename them 'modern sporting rifles.' However, assault rifles available to civilians are almost identical to the military versions (Military.com, 2023). They do not just look alike. Both versions can fire the same high-velocity bullets designed to efficiently kill humans (Bartlett & Helfet, 2000).

Civilian assault rifles can convert to near full or fully automatic machine guns anyway. Many of us are familiar with the horrific effects of such modifications from the infamous 2017 Las Vegas mass shooting. In ten minutes, one deranged perpetrator mercilessly fired one thousand bullets into an outdoor concert from a hotel window above (Trotta, 2017).

Nevertheless, it cannot be overemphasized that despite the increased killing capacity of assault rifles, many more Americans are killed with handguns. We must strictly regulate dangerous assault rifles, but we cannot take our focus away from regulating all firearms regardless of size, shape, or magazine capacity. That is like saying we should ban sports cars. All cars must obey traffic laws. Many more people are killed in ordinary sedans than in sports cars.

If the AR15 was federally banned today, there would be an AR15.1 tomorrow. In fact, in States where assault rifles are banned, there is a huge market for "State-compliant AR15s" (Eckholm,

2015). These are easily modified assault rifles that evade local restrictions. They can also be easily changed back to the original AR15 design after you buy the State compliant version.

You can even purchase a "featureless AR15" (Eckholm, 2015). That's like buying a family car with a racing engine. It does not look like a military weapon but is for all practical purposes.

Alternatively, you can buy gun 'kits' that don't have serial numbers and don't require background checks. They are manufactured to only about 80%, so they are not legally considered "firearms." The customer buys them and quickly finishes the other 20% with little skill required. They are called ghost guns. There's nothing ephemeral about them. These are real guns, albeit without serial numbers. It's like buying a car without a back seat to avoid having to register it. You buy it, take it home, and just put a back seat in it yourself.

State-compliant assault rifles, featureless assault rifles, and ghost guns are examples of the gun industry's clever responses to our feeble gun laws. By now, you should understand why I keep repeating: We must comprehensively regulate all

WHY I NO LONGER CARRY

firearms regardless of how they look or operate. We need fewer guns, not just more gun laws.

GUNAHOLIC

BULLET POINT 6

ARE GUN RIGHTS UNLIMITED?

No. And Firearm Regulations Are Constitutional

The Second Amendment of the Constitution was ratified on December 15, 1791. It reads: "A well regulated Militia, being necessary to the security of a free State, the right of the people to keep and bear

Arms, shall not be infringed" (U.S. Const. amend. II).

Despite typos and grammatical errors, the Second Amendment guarantees the right "to keep and bear Arms" (Loesch, 2014). However, it does not specify 'who' gets that right. What the Second Amendment says has been subject to interpretation over the years.

However, we all can agree on what the Second Amendment did 'not' say:

- **It did not say "the people" outside "well regulated Militia" are included.**

- **It did not say if "the people" applied to individuals.**

- **It did not say anything about "concealed carry."**

- **It did not say what type of "Arms" were protected.**

- **It did not say "infringed" excluded limits.**

- **It did not say if "Arms" and ammo could be kept at home.**

What it does say is endlessly debated, but I advise you to avoid crawling down that rabbit hole. With no final authoritative interpretation, the meaning of the Second Amendment changes with our current understandings throughout history (Austin, 2013) (Colajuta, 2022) (Cornell, 2008) (DeBrabander, 2015) (Franks, 2019) (Thoreau, 2018) (Spitzer, 2017) (Waldman, 2015) (Winkler, 2011).

However, we 'do' know that the Militia was "well regulated," and gun regulations existed from America's founding. Gun regulations were a carryover from British common law. In early America, militiamen had their muskets regularly inspected and were fined if they violated militia standards. Loyalty pledges to the government were also required to own a firearm (Spitzer, 2017). That is a far cry from owning a gun to protect oneself from our own 'tyrannical' government.

There were restrictions on armed traveling, especially in towns or cities. Several had restrictions on concealed carry. Concealing a handgun was often looked upon as a "cowardly practice" by those with an "improper, aggressive motive" (Meltzer, 2014). As such, there were bans on pistols since they were easier to hide than muskets. (Note: The definition of "pistol" and "handgun" changed over time.)

Even gunpowder was restricted and feared as a fire hazard (Stephenson, 1925). Many places banned keeping gunpowder or ammunition inside your home. Today's firefighters are increasingly vigilant not just for people trapped in fires, but for ammo and especially loaded (chambered) firearms (Tamme, 2015).

Gunpowder and ammunition were kept in storage houses. These stone structures were called "magazines," hence today's namesake gun accessory. Firearms were also stored in these magazine buildings (Murphey, 2000).

Those are just some of the more common regulations from the early days of America. And more recently, the late conservative Justice Scalia of the U.S. Supreme Court reminded us, "Like most rights, the right secured by the Second Amendment is not unlimited" (U.S. Supreme Court, 2008).

Those who adhere to an "originalist" view of the Constitution should note that we 'originally' had firearm, gunpowder, and ammunition regulations. Today, gun regulations are frowned upon as un-American by many. That is a mistaken and deadly misunderstanding of American tradition and history.

The Second Amendment is not the problem – it's our misunderstanding. The right to bear arms can only work alongside regulations as it always has (Austin, 2013) (Spitzer, 2017) (U.S. Supreme Court, 2008). Furthermore, as times change, our laws and regulations can be updated per the "Necessary and Proper Clause" of the U.S. Constitution (Constitution.gov, 2013).

That does not require changing or amending the Constitution. Nevertheless, by keeping our laws current and relevant we can be faithful to the Constitution, and better protect "Life, Liberty and the pursuit of Happiness" for all, as found in our Declaration of Independence (Cornell, 2008).

GUNAHOLIC

BULLET POINT 7

DO GUNS AFFECT THE BORDER?

Yes, Our Guns Arm the Cartels

Mexico, Central America, and the Caribbean are ravaged by drug cartels armed with American guns. As our firearms are trafficked south, migrants are trafficked north (Detty, 2013) (Grillo, 2021) (Mineo, 2022) (Pane, 2018).

Some bury their loved ones before making these notoriously dangerous journeys. Cartels and gangs with USA-made weapons break into homes to kill, rape, and take over entire neighborhoods (Grillo, 2021) (Pane, 2018). Human traffickers are seen brazenly carrying American AR15s 'inside' the United States along the border. Cartels expanded their operations across the United States (U.S. Drug Enforcement Administration, 2015).

Mexico recently sued US gun manufacturers for $10 billion for facilitating gun trafficking to the cartels. A US federal judge dismissed that lawsuit, and Mexico appealed (Morland, 2023). Mexico followed up with another case against US gun dealers located on the US side of the border (Associated Press, 2022). At least 200,000 to 250,000 US guns are trafficked across the border yearly as manufacturers, politicians, and US courts look the other way (Government Accountability Office, 2021) (McDougal, 2013) (Mineo, 2022).

If you have time, look up Ciudad Juarez, Mexico on a map. It's one of several border cities where drug cartels are headquartered. Then search "nearby gun stores." You will not find a single gun store anywhere near Ciudad Juarez – in Mexico. However, in nearby El Paso, Texas, you will see a cluster of gun stores right along the border and within walking distance of the Juarez Cartel.

US gun stores are conveniently located along the border to sell weapons to cartels. They sell to legal buyers (straw purchasers, as mentioned) who transfer them to the cartels. It's not difficult for these or other gun stores to bypass US gun laws.

When was the last time a gun dealer was prosecuted for trafficking guns to Mexico? It is not as if ATF agents aren't making arrests. They are not aggressively prosecuted due to politics and the gun lobby. Gun traffickers simply fill their cars or vans with firearms and drive them across the border to drug cartels and their associates.

Cartels in Mexico and Central America outgun their police and military. Drug cartels control various government segments and have more money and power than large US corporations and even a few countries.

As agriculture and other businesses shift to selling illicit drugs and economies are destroyed, millions continue to lose jobs (Pane, 2018). Children are trafficked regularly for sex, used as drug couriers, and forced to do other work for cartels (U.S. Drug Enforcement Administration, 2021). Parents have little choice but to flee. Some are not given a choice and are smuggled into the USA as sex slaves and for forced labor.

Some wonder how a mother could pay human traffickers to take her children with or without her through jungles, deserts, and rivers to reach America. However, she dreads not sending them away from the home village ravaged by cartels and gangs – all enabled by American firearms.

I am not endorsing illegal immigration. But please. Let's look at the strong link between American firearms and border crossings before we malign anyone for doing what they must do to survive. There is more involved than firearms, but American guns are a critical factor in the border crisis.

In summary, we cannot effectively control border crossings without halting the trafficking of American firearms.

BULLET POINT 8

SECOND AMENDMENT & TYRANNY

It Originally Concerned British Tyranny

The Second Amendment provides for a well-regulated militia "necessary to the security of a free State." Some insist that this clause protects Americans against our government turned tyrannical (Cooter, 2022) (McCord, 2021) (Pason, 2021).

GUNAHOLIC

The Second Amendment may protect us from tyrannical government, but it was not essentially to protect us from our government. Soon after the Revolutionary War ended and the Second Amendment was ratified, we fought England again in the War of 1812. It was that British government we most feared, not our government of "we the people" (US Constitution, 2023).

We also feared other foreign tyrannical 'governments' but not their people or even soldiers per se. We have it backward; our Constitution did not. Destroy a tyrannical government and not its people. The world does not have to kill millions of young draftees and allow for "collateral damage" of innocent civilians to destroy one tyrannical government. Our world has the finances, arms, resources, and military capacity to destroy any aggressive and deadly government. However, we lack the collective will to destroy tyrannical governments. Death tolls rise as rogue leaders inflict mass casualties around the world. We would rather bomb their soldiers for years on end than cut the snake's head off.

Had the founders designed the militia to protect us from our government, they indeed would 'not' have named the head of our government to lead it! The Constitution put the US President as Commander in Chief of the militia: "**The President shall be Commander** in Chief of the Army and Navy of the United States, and of the Militia of the several States …" (US Constitution, 2023).

The Constitution also gave Congress the power "To provide for calling forth the Militia to execute the Laws of the Union, suppress Insurrections and repel Invasions; To provide for organizing, arming, and disciplining, the Militia …" (Ibid.).

That is, the Constitution did not intend for our militia to destroy our own government that we had just formed. The Constitution even put our government 'in charge' of the militia and did not intend for the militia to destroy itself.

Our militia even helped to suppress armed insurrections in the founding years. One was Shays' Rebellion. That armed uprising began as a tax revolt. Militia were called to suppress it. The militia members had divided loyalties and were unregulated. Some sided with the insurrectionists

(Massachusetts Historical Society, 2013). That and similar disorderly insurrections provided the backdrop to the "well Regulated" part of the Second Amendment. We saw what an unregulated militia could do, which was not good. Therefore, the Second Amendment specified a "well Regulated" militia.

The Constitution contains the "Necessary and Proper Clause," as mentioned in another context, to grant our government the authority to enact future laws and regulations. This permits Congress to pass future laws as needed: "To make all Laws which shall be necessary and proper for carrying into Execution the foregoing Powers, and all other Powers vested by this Constitution in the Government of the United States, or in any Department or Officer thereof" (Cooter, 2022) (US Constitution, 2023).

The Constitution, therefore, ensures there is nothing to prevent our government from issuing new laws and regulations to live up to the Preamble of the US Constitution: "We the People of the United States, in Order to form a more perfect Union, establish Justice, insure domestic Tranquility, provide for the common defense, promote the general Welfare, and secure the Blessings of Liberty to ourselves and our Posterity, do ordain and establish this Constitution for the United States of America" (US Constitution, 2023).

GUNAHOLIC

WHY I NO LONGER CARRY

BULLET POINT 9

ARE GUNS A "GOD-GIVEN" RIGHT?

There's No Mention of That in The Bible

Before I entered the police department in New York City, I studied theology and intended to enter the clergy. I later regretted studying theology since I never used it professionally. Though I'm not a theologian, my studies later proved somewhat helpful concerning gun violence:

GUNAHOLIC

Many pro-gun advocates quote the Bible out of context to fit their beliefs. Even the local priest in my childhood parish in the Bronx concealed-carried a 38-caliber snub nose revolver (then a popular police off-duty handgun). I asked him why he carried a gun, and he answered, "Because I work in these tough neighborhoods." Our section of the Bronx and Yonkers had relatively low crime, which is beside the point.

Some years later, in the police department, I noticed that one of our surgeons carried a Smith & Wesson 29 Revolver. That's one of the most powerful handguns, and officers were prohibited from carrying them. He walked around police department buildings with a stethoscope around his neck and a 44 magnum on his waistband.

The priest and the surgeon have no less of a right to defend themselves, but it still makes you wonder how our minds rationalize what we do. Sorry if I am off base, but the priest and doctor carrying handguns were like nails sticking out of plywood. They routinely attended to gunshot victims and wiped tears from grieving moms and loved ones.

WHY I NO LONGER CARRY

I am not judging anyone personally. They undoubtedly helped many more people than I alone ever could. I am just pointing out that we can bend the Second Amendment, Bible verses, and even the Hippocratic oath to fit personal views. Twisting the Second Amendment and sacred verses out of context has historically proved divisive and fatal.

The Christian part of the Holy Bible (aka 'New Testament') does not mention a "God-given right" to arms, as some claim. There may be Biblical support for self-defense, but that's not the same as a God-given right to bear arms. It also contradicts Christ's teachings about forgiving our enemies and turning the other cheek (Giles, 2021).

There is mention of warfare in the Jewish Bible (aka Hebrew Bible, Torah, or Christian 'Old Testament' – please pardon this simplification of labels). However, the 'God-given right to bear arms' comes primarily from famous Christian gun rights advocates who quote Bible verses out of context (Atwood, 2012). For this reason, I focus on the Christian part of the Bible.

The Jewish and Christian Bibles are complementary in the message of love. However, Christians are taught to prioritize the Christian 'New Testament' (written as the new "covenant"). The Christian Bible reads, "But in fact the ministry Jesus has received is as superior to theirs as the covenant of which he is mediator is superior to the old one, since the new covenant is established on better promises" (Hebrews 8:6).

That implies not that the New Testament is superior to the Old Testament in its core principles, but that Christ renewed certain teachings. "He has made everything beautiful in its time..." (Ecclesiastes 3:11). Christians are taught to defer to the New Testament and not selectively reach back into the Old Testament to fit personal views.

The Old Testament message of "an eye for an eye" (Exodus 21:24) was fitting in Biblical times with very different means of justice. However, Christ later taught, "You have heard that it was said, 'Eye for eye and tooth for tooth.' But I tell you not to resist an evil person. If someone slaps you on your right cheek, turn to him the other also" (Matthew 5:38-39).

Christ also annulled the critical Old Testament laws of divorce and the Sabbath. "By calling this covenant 'new,' he has made the first one obsolete" (Hebrews 8:13, see 2 Cor 3). Due to health concerns, dietary and cleanliness laws made more sense in past years. These laws were also changed in the time of Christ. The core messages remained unchanged across religious history, but peripheral laws were adapted to the times. Unfortunately, we often fight over our different religious traditions and lose sight of the core principles that are essentially the same.

Likewise, swords are mentioned more in the Old Testament, but Christ later taught His disciples, "Put your sword back in its place ... for all who draw the sword will die by the sword." (Matthew 26:52). Gun rights advocates often read "swords" out of context and ignore that command. They like to quote Luke 22:36. But reputable Christian Bible scholars explain that Luke 22:36 fulfills specific prophecies and is not a license to be armed (Barrigar, 2023) (Keddie, 2023) (Okoronkwo, 2014).

Many other verses are read out of historical context. We've seen this not only with guns but with slavery and the oppression of women. Many found justification for slavery in the Bible. Others still find excuses to oppress women. Women and men are equal as human beings. The problem is not scripture but our inability to find meaning outside the historical framework.

Gun rights advocates often smear US politicians who do not hold their pro-gun views. Some devout Christians on both sides of gun politics denigrate politicians on the other side. The Bible specifically warns against this: "Let everyone be subject to the governing authorities … whoever rebels against the authority is rebelling against what God has instituted …" (Romans 13:1-2).

Regardless of party, this back-and-forth trashing of politicians is red meat for America's adversaries overseas and at home. Mainstream media on both 'sides' belittle the other side in full view of the world. Americans should get involved in our local and national communities and vote. However, we should not rebel against our government. If we do not like who is in office, we should keep voting or get more involved. That's how we have always done it. Though not perfect, it's still far better than disrespecting our government. It's almost like complaining about our own family to neighbors.

Consult, discuss, and even complain civilly and protest, but don't rebel.

The Bible has a 'Second Commandment' – not a 'Second Amendment.' The Second Commandment tells us to worship God and not idols. We are advised not to worship false Gods. Many cannot imagine giving up their guns.

Whether or not you worship guns as an "idol," Isaiah 2:4 nonetheless calls us to beat our "swords into plowshares." Isaiah not only addresses 'nations' as some assume, but people individually ("many people").

I write to the devout Christian gun rights advocate: Remember those who rebelled against Christ. They were the most learned in the Bible. Those who sacrificed their all for Christ and followed Him included ordinary and unlearned fishermen and the struggling masses, even the downcast. They saw something that the learned doctors of the law could not. Can you give up your daily carry weapon? Is the Second Amendment more important than the Second Commandment? Do you revere the Constitution over the Bible? The Constitution has amendments, but the Bible does not.

GUNAHOLIC

"Whoever has ears, let them hear" (Matthew 11:15).

WHY I NO LONGER CARRY

BULLET POINT 10

DOES RESEARCH SUPPORT GUNS?

"Industry-Sponsored" Research Does

I want to start this section by drawing similarities between gun industry-sponsored research and research sponsored by the tobacco and alcohol industries:

Years ago, tobacco research said cigarettes were healthy. Next up was the alcohol industry. They paid for 'favorable' research to conclude that drinking benefits you. That has been widely discredited (Pelc C, 2021). The CDC says, "The less alcohol you drink, the lower your risk for cancer" (CDC, 2023). Drinking is linked to heart problems and even wrinkling (American College of Cardiology, 2016) (Cimons, 2023) (Zhao J, 2023). Similarly, pro-gun research promotes that guns make us safer (Hemenway D, 2015) (Henigan, 2016). Thankfully, real science eventually prevails.

Nonetheless, Supreme Court justices sometimes fall victim to biased gun research. So much unscientific gun research is circulating. Some end up in amicus curiae briefs presented to the justices as they deliberate on gun laws. We suffer the consequences.

For an example of biased gun research, I will briefly review a popular and typical pro-gun book: "The War on Guns: Arming Yourself Against Gun Control Lies" (Lott, 2016). Newsweek Magazine described the author as "The Gun Crowd's Guru" (Bai, 2001). I will review that seminal and influential pro-gun book to highlight some common biases (Gun Violence Research, 2023) (Hargis, 2019). (Note: Biases are also found in research from gun-control advocates.)

This is not a personal attack on the author, whom I will not name beyond the citation. Just know he is very popular with the NRA and the broader gun culture. He authored briefs for the Supreme Court before they ruled on important gun cases.

He began his book with a misleading statement: He wrote that the Supreme Court decided "the government can't simply ban people from owning guns." That may be technically correct since he included "simply" and is vague, but it is otherwise false. As mentioned, even the majority Court opinion by the late Justice Scalia wrote that "the Second Amendment is not unlimited. … (it is) not a right to keep and carry any weapon whatsoever in any manner whatsoever and for whatever purpose" (U.S. Supreme Court, 2008).

For an expert witness who gets the ear of the Supreme Court, he gets many firearms basics wrong: He wrote, "civilian versions of the AR-15 and AK-47 (aka "assault rifles") are like military guns in their cosmetics, but not in the way they operate." Again, he is only technically correct. As mentioned before, many standard-issue military rifles are semiautomatic. They are not all 'fully' automatic machine guns, as he implied. He wrote that assault rifles (".223-caliber bullets") "are best for hunting small game animals." I hunted small game years ago and know it is not a good bullet for that purpose. Ask any hunter.

He wrote, "High-capacity magazines also have a greater chance of jamming." Again, he is only technically correct. The odds of most high-capacity magazines jamming are virtually the same as standard-capacity magazines.

Here is where he crossed the line: He wrote, "Young children can't simply fire a typical semi-auto pistol." That is false and irresponsible. He said children are not at an increased risk of gun accidents because "Few are likely to know that the slide needs to be pulled back to put a bullet in the chamber." False again. A child does not need to load the next bullet into a chamber – pistols do that for you – hence the term semiautomatic. That also implies that the pistol is sitting around unloaded. Many, if not most, who keep firearms at home for self-defense keep at least one gun fully loaded and unlocked (Anglemyer, 2014) (Hoskins K, 2020) (Kellermann AL, 1998) (Lee LK, 2022) (Mauri, 2019) (Miller M, 2022). The child merely needs to pull the trigger like a toy gun.

The deception continues: He wrote that young children "may not be aware that the safety has to be switched off." However, most pistols sold in America do not have manual trigger safeties. He is repeatedly proven false and grossly irresponsible with senseless and unnecessary accidental gun deaths of many children and adults.

He suggested that even "the elderly" keep guns at home and wrote, "Without a gun, my mother would have no realistic means of defending himself." I do not know where she lived and cannot judge his mother's or anyone's risk of danger, regardless of age. Nevertheless, he ignored reputable research that concluded guns at home increase the chances of family members dying (Kellermann AL, 1998) (Lee LK, 2022). Additional research he omitted focuses on America's increasing demographic of elderly gun owners with dementia (Spangenberg, 2015) (Tonetti L, 2022) (Youngblood, 2022).

The US leads the developed world in mass shootings. Nevertheless, he created his own version of mass shootings – defining them with "at least fifteen" victims. Mass shootings are commonly considered four or more victims, not fifteen (Chmielewski, 2023). That alone left out most mass shootings in the US. He even included civil wars in the foreign 'mass shooting' numbers.

He excluded gang-related mass shootings in the USA. That is like saying inner city youth do not deserve to be counted (Lazar, 2022) (Peterson, 2021). He counted "Europe," "Africa," and "India/Pakistan" as single countries and failed to mention that Europe has about double the US population. He makes every statistical error to make America look like we have fewer mass shootings.

He said the media undercounts 'defensive gun use' (DGU), where legally armed citizens use their guns to defend themselves. Researchers challenged his unrealistically high numbers. He could not provide a valid source. He claimed he 'lost' his survey data (Gun Violence Research, 2023) (Hargis, 2019). He also left out the alternative: If armed citizens use their guns, why isn't he counting armed criminals?

'Offensive gun use' can be found in scholarly research had he looked (Wright, 2008).

There are many other research errors. As with many pro-gun books, articles, and amicus curiae briefs, it resembles gun marketing brochures but not scientific research (Gun Violence Research, 2023) (Hargis, 2019).

GUNAHOLIC

WHY I NO LONGER CARRY

BULLET POINT 11

DO MORE GUNS = LESS CRIME?

That's Another Gun Myth

This fools both gun rights and gun control advocates. Like stocks, crime goes up and down. However, the number of guns only goes up. Old guns are not thrown out with the trash. Millions of new firearms are sold annually in America (ATF,

2021). Add these to the hundreds of millions already owned. Gun owners die; their guns do not. We have more guns than people, and gun ownership crosses all demographics (Parker K. H., 2017).

Crime rates in America are down from past peaks. For example, Chicago and NYC had more crime in the 1980s and early 1990s (FBI UCR Chicago, 2023) (FBI UCR NYC, 2023). Both cities are safer today. However, crime and homicide remain high in specific neighborhoods (Gullion, 2022) (NYPD, 2023). States with the most lenient gun laws also have more violent crimes and firearm mortality than other States (CDC Firearm Mortality, 2023) (Kaufman EJ, 2018). Even though 'overall' crime is down in America, more people are killed with guns than ever before (Gramlich, 2023). Whether guns are used in high-crime neighborhoods or in lenient gun States, where there are more guns, there are more gun deaths.

Industry-sponsored researchers highlight specific years when general crime rates temporarily decreased and say, "Look, more guns and less crime." They conveniently overlook when crime goes up again. They also ignore gun hotspots. They choose high crime years in the 1980s and early

1990s that coincided with the crack cocaine epidemic. They compare that against subsequent lower crime years to draw false causation between more guns and less crime. That is not research – it is gun marketing (Powell J L, 2020) (Henigan, 2016).

Nevertheless, crime has been on a relative rise again since 2015. They fix that by ending their crime chart before 2015 to keep to their narrative that "more guns = less crime." Many of us don't have the time to catch this fraud. Scholarly research will (sometimes) find it. Unfortunately, that is usually after the disinformation spreads, even to the Supreme Court.

Crime has been around since the beginning of humankind. More guns do not always equal less (or more) crime per se, but more gun homicides, accidental shootings, and suicides: the more guns, the more gun deaths. Especially in disadvantaged areas (Braga A. A., 2021) and States with lenient gun laws.

If you have time, do an Internet search on gun homicides and gun suicides over time. You will discover that the more guns, the more gun deaths, regardless of short-term increases or decreases in other crimes (Braga A. A., 2021) (Semenza, 2022) (Cukier, 2002).

Please do not rely on research by others, no matter what their views. Bias affects all of us. Both pro-gun and gun control advocates twist stats. You can find higher crime rates in other countries. However, you cannot find higher gun homicide rates in 'comparable' countries (Gramlich, 2023) (Hemenway & Miller, 2000). Unless researchers arbitrarily change their research criteria to skew statistics, as mentioned in (Hargis, 2019) (Mascia, 2021).

Take, for example, the Virgin Islands. Half of the Virgin Islands are American (USVI), and half are British (BVI). Both have "moderate" levels of crime per the World Bank (The World Bank - BVI, 2023) (The World Bank - USVI, 2023). Their customs are similar, and friends and family live and work in both nations. Ferries shuttle US and British citizens back and forth. The British islands even use the US Dollar as their 'official' currency since the economy is so intertwined.

WHY I NO LONGER CARRY

I have been to both island nations to visit friends. There are many similarities. However, the US islands have the Second Amendment and easy access to guns. The British islands do not. The difference is not so much the general crime rate but homicides. The well-armed US islands have over 5X more homicides (ibid.). Not more crime, but more gun deaths. You will not see this relevant comparison in any pro-gun 'research.'

Other examples confirm that "homicides increase" with violent crime when there are more guns (Donohue, 2022). Don't be fooled by false comparisons between guns and general crime rates or by hand-picked years or locations.

Remember what matters most: More guns = more gun deaths (Donohue J. J., 2022).

GUNAHOLIC

BULLET POINT 12

ARE LAWS UNFAIR TO GUN OWNERS?

No. Legal Owners Are the Source of Illegal Guns

There would be virtually no illegal guns without legal guns. Most guns start their lives legally (Vinzant, 2015). More than one thousand guns are reported 'stolen' each day (Hemenway D. A., 2017). These numbers are staggering.

Total estimates of lost or stolen guns are as high as 380,000 each year (Hemenway, 2017). That doesn't include the hundreds of thousands more trafficked yearly across the Southern border to drug cartels (Associated Press, 2022).

Why are most gun thefts concentrated in just a few Southern States (ATF, 2023)? Do northern States not have thieves? They surely do. However, these Southern States are located at the starting line of the gun trafficking route to the north. These guns are not simply 'stolen' more in the South. Many are 'reported' stolen to disassociate their serial numbers from the original owners, who sell them into illegal gun markets up north and elsewhere.

Profit estimates vary for these legal-to-illegal gun sales, but several are around 50%. No limit exists on how many firearms you can purchase or report stolen. You can buy as many firearms as you can fit in your car, report them stolen, and drive north to get rich.

Most firearms are 'reported' stolen from parked cars (O'Toole, 2022). The top five states where guns are 'stolen' are all in the South. Strangely, none of these States rank top in auto theft (NICB, 2022). The State with the highest rate of gun theft is Mississippi (for the years researched). However, Mississippi has a comparatively low auto theft rate and ranks low in larceny overall (Statista, 2023).

So why are so many firearms 'stolen' from cars in the relatively low theft State of Mississippi? Moreover, if countless guns are stolen from vehicles in Mississippi, why would gun owners leave them in cars? (I've visited and have longtime friends from Mississippi. This is to make a point and not malign the people of Mississippi.)

It is because Mississippi, Alabama, and other Southern States are the primary source of illegal firearms heading to cities such as Baltimore, Philadelphia, New York, and Washington, DC. The cities have strict gun laws and offer high profits for illegal gun sales. Illegal guns trafficked north is called the "Iron Pipeline" (Braga, 2021).

Mississippi does not mysteriously have more thieves; it just has unscrupulous gun owners reselling legal firearms into illegal gun markets. They're not the only ones doing this. All legal guns must be regulated much more carefully.

If your cars keep getting stolen, you will not find an insurance company to underwrite such lousy luck or gross irresponsibility. The same should apply to having your lethal weapons lost or stolen. As with our other gun laws, insurance restrictions alone will not prevent most gun violence (Gilles, 2013). Furthermore, it may even increase gun casualties if it delays much-needed gun reform.

In summary, one of the most effective ways to control illegal guns is to regulate legal guns strictly. There must be stringent background checks, gun registries, and consequences for loss or theft, as in the automobile insurance industry.

BULLET POINT 13

WHAT AGENCY REGULATES GUNS?

None

Firearms are the "only" consumer product not regulated by the federal government for health or safety. Toy guns are regulated for safety, but real guns are not! You may read that again. In fact, please do.

GUNAHOLIC

The Consumer Product Safety Commission (CPSC) prohibits the government from regulating one of our most dangerous consumer products – firearms (CPSC, 2023) (Barton, 2023). No federal oversight agency can ban hazardous firearms or even recall defective ones. The gun industry designs weapons for lethality without having to incorporate safety features (Violence Policy Center, 2023).

Additionally, no federal agency regulates firearms for noise pollution, including noise at firing ranges. Noise from gunshots can damage the hearing of shooters, nearby residents, and wildlife (Bhatt, 2017) (Murphy WJ, 2007).

The same applies to toxic lead pollution (Chen, 2011) (Sanderson, 2018). When pistols and rifles are fired at outdoor ranges, poisonous levels of lead are continually dumped into the soil and water supplies (Hall-Gale, 2014) (Hockmann K, 2015) (Sanderson, 2018).

Even simple safety features on firearms are typically frowned upon by gun owners. They are especially disliked by those who carry for self-defense. They want their carry weapons ready to kill instantly without wasting time turning off a manual trigger lock or similar safety device. You should not carry a firearm if you cannot quickly unlock a trigger.

Federal regulators would not approve most gun models on the market today. The gun lobby persuaded Congress to exempt manufacturers from incorporating even basic safety features. Untold numbers of accidental deaths are the result (Gramlich, 2023) (The Trace, 2022).

The Protection of Lawful Commerce in Arms Act (PLCAA) also broadly protects firearms manufacturers from litigation. Gun manufacturers are not liable for making unsafe guns or for damages. In addition, the PLCAA protects gun manufacturers and dealers from many negligent sales practices that contribute to illegal firearms and thousands of deaths every year (109th Congress, 2005) (Stempel, 2021).

If you are not familiar with firearms, remember this: Most pistols sold in America do not have manual trigger safeties. Even those with nominal 'safeties' – such as Glock's "Trigger Safety" – do not prevent them from firing. I will reference Glock's website here if you want to see for yourself how unsafe their "trigger safety" really is (Glock, 2023). If you pull the Glock trigger, it fires. It's the epitome of legal deception and not gun safety.

Those unfamiliar with pistols, particularly Glocks, can easily be fooled into believing Glock triggers have manual trigger locks. Nevertheless, it fires when a child or anyone pulls it. Ask any Glock or other pistol owner if they would trust their child with their Glock "Trigger Safety." No! They do not have safe triggers, no matter what they call them.

Here is another shocker: A Glock's trigger must be pulled to clean the pistol! Specifically, its trigger must be pulled to "fieldstrip" it and expose its internal parts for cleaning. There have been unintentional discharges of Glock pistols during this hazardous cleaning process. Pistol owners, family, and friends have been injured or killed during this cleaning process (The Trace, 2022) (Solnick, 2019).

Most pistols can be fired even after their magazines are 'removed.' If there is still a bullet in the pistol's chamber, removing the magazine does not remove that bullet. It's easy to forget your pistol is loaded after you remove its magazine. Add to that an aging demographic of gun owners in America (Pinholt, 2014) (Spangenberg, 2015).

A few brands voluntarily ensure that it is impossible to fire their firearms without their magazines inserted. That's wise, but it's not a legal requirement or very common. It can also confuse gun owners who own several pistols – some will fire, and some will not. We're taught to assume all guns are loaded and point them in a safe direction. But we are also taught to drive safely. Accidents happen even to the most cautious.

Firearm safety hazards are numerous. These were just some of the more deadly product safety hazards that result from the industry's exemptions from federal safety standards and liability.

GUNAHOLIC

BULLET POINT 14

IS IT OKAY TO KEEP GUNS HOME?

That Depends, But It's Also a Hazard

Surveys show that gun owners, particularly those who own guns for defense, commonly keep at least one loaded gun readily accessible (Carter, 2022) (Mauri, 2019) (Weil DS, 1992). Surveys aside, I used to, and most gun owners I know, walk around their homes fully armed. They also keep at least one loaded firearm within easy reach of their bed when sleeping.

Most reading this book already understand the dangers of loaded firearms at home. This section is about less-known safety hazards:

Would you set your alarm for 3 AM and immediately start your car and drive? Probably not. You would splash some water on your face or maybe have a cup of coffee to try to wake up. It takes up to an hour for our brains to fully function after waking.

That brain delay is known in neurology as "sleep inertia" (Trotti, 2017). The CDC defines it as "a temporary disorientation and decline in performance and/or mood after awakening from sleep." The CDC explains that just after waking, the average person "can show slower reaction time, poorer short-term memory, and slower speed of thinking, reasoning, remembering, and learning" (CDC, 2021).

Now, mix sleep inertia with loaded firearms. Also, factor in an aging population of gun owners and dementia (Tonetti L, 2022) (Youngblood, 2022). Even nursing homes and assisted care facilities allow firearms if not posted or against the law. Is that a burglar at your door or a stranded driver? Is it a threat, or is someone knocking on the wrong door? Maybe it's a family member coming home and trying not to wake you. Or perhaps it's a neighbor with cognitive or developmental challenges. You've probably seen news of homeowners accidentally shooting someone at their door or in their driveway.

It is more the exception than the rule that a homeowner will ever need a firearm for home defense. Peer-reviewed research concludes, "Guns kept in homes are more likely to be involved in a fatal or nonfatal accidental shooting, criminal assault, or suicide attempt than to be used to injure or kill in self-defense" (Kellermann AL, 1998).

Similar studies show the same results. For example, other peer-reviewed research found "little evidence that self-defense gun use is uniquely beneficial in reducing the likelihood of injury" and "many of the claims about the benefits of gun ownership are largely myths" (Hemenway D, 2015) (Henigan, 2016).

Additional peer-reviewed research found that anyone, especially women, living with handgun owners is more than twice as likely to die from homicide or suicide (Miller M, 2022) (Anglemyer, 2014). Despite widespread perceptions that guns at home provide security, credible studies suggest people who live in homes with firearms are at a higher risk of gun death (Moyer, 2020) (Studdert, 2022).

While some may need a lethal weapon to defend themselves, studies confirm it is best to call the police. Multiple surveys underscore the misconception that civilians commonly fire guns in self-defense (Hemenway D, 2015). Did you or anyone you know ever fire a gun in self-defense?

Now, ask if you know anyone injured, killed, or committed suicide with a firearm. I bet you can name more in the latter category. I can, even after responding to many confirmed shootings.

WHY I NO LONGER CARRY

BULLET POINT 15

IS MOST CRIME BLACK-ON-BLACK?

No. That's Misleading & Ripe for Racism

(This bullet point, in particular, was written as a cohesive chapter. Therefore, reading or quoting sentences out of context may not accurately reflect the intended meaning.)

Some gun rights advocates write in books and even research papers that crime is mostly Black-on-Black. Not only is that false, but it is misleading. Unscrupulous researchers report either 'total' crimes, or crime 'rates' (per race) – depending on which number they want to exaggerate. Bias in reporting quantitative data results (Isbell, 2022).

Those who want to show that Blacks commit more crime stress the (sometimes) higher Black crime 'rate.' They fail to mention that Whites commit more crimes overall. Most crime is White-on-White. Almost 70% of those arrested are White. Most "Violent crime" is also White-on-White. (FBI, Arrests by Race and Ethnicity Table 43, 2019) (FBI, Expanded Homicide Data Table 6, 2019) (Morgan, 2022).

The latter is rarely spoken about in the gun rights literature. It does not matter what color a criminal is. Many gun rights researchers unscientifically imply that crime is related to being Black (Nasheed, 2020). They say it stems from "broken" Black families. They like to blame "deadbeat Black fathers." They assume Whites don't get divorced or separated. Indeed, Whites get divorced and separated in much greater numbers than Blacks.

They omit that most families with single mothers are White (NCES, 2023) (Finances Online, 2023). Total White single-parent families have more than doubled since 1970 (Department of Justice, 2023). That's the highest increase of all demographics. I point this out to show the biases in gun research, not to judge anyone's family structure.

Regardless of statistics, bullets do not see color. Blacks are disproportionately involved in crime by population size. However, in statistics, "correlation is not causation." Many large cities have higher proportions of Blacks and other minorities. That often results in disproportionate crime rates. When you have more disadvantaged environments, regardless of color or ethnicity, there is typically increased crime (Hannon, 2005). You can more accurately say most crime is "disadvantaged on disadvantaged." Color is not statistically causative.

(Being disadvantaged also does not "cause" crime, and many of the world's most outstanding individuals are/were disadvantaged.)

Disadvantaged, predominately White areas can also have more crime than our national averages (Philips, 2002). Crime is influenced by factors such as poverty, unemployment, substandard education, and drugs, including one of the most prevalent drugs associated with crime: alcohol. Watch the television series Cops and see how many police interactions involve drunkenness. Blacks may commit crimes at higher rates in some cities, but being Black is not a cause of crime, including gun crime (Hannon, 2005) (Philips, 2002).

Urban areas often have higher police budgets and more Black residents. With more police on patrol, the number of Black arrests rises. That's math, not color. It is also the epitome of structural racism in that people of color disproportionately live in more challenging environments.

Some less scrupulous police officers (of all colors) add to these social injustices and structural racism. They make discretionary late-shift arrests or car stops to bolster their overtime pay (Olmstead, 2018) (Moskos, 2008). It is important to note that this is not proof of racism by the individual arresting officer. Nevertheless, it is an example of structural racism that helps keep us divided. Those who say, "Blacks get arrested more," should know that much more is happening than is apparent.

The easy fix right before us is disconnecting overtime pay from arrests. It's easy but requires legislation and the will to change how things are done. It is also an easy way to weed out bad cops, keep good cops safer, and prevent injustices in the community. Note that the discretionary arrests are still legal and valid. Nevertheless, they occur more frequently in neighborhoods with more police (of all colors) on patrol and less in the suburbs.

The cops I know are not more or less racist than our broader society, and no color lacks prejudice. My family is of mixed race, ethnicity, and religion. The inner-city Bronx high school I attended years ago is similarly diverse. My social circles are also diverse. I have seen prejudice equally committed regardless of color or ethnicity.

However, I've seen horrific "racism" perpetrated against people of color. Racism involves not just prejudice but 'dehumanizing' someone based on their 'race.' Biologically and genetically, there is one human race. Moreover, in other parts of the world, the demographics of racism change according to who has the power. My friend, born in Nigeria, taught me about the "racism" involving people from one local Nigerian tribe against the other. He said it was as equally dehumanizing as racism in America. There is no racism 'gene.' We all have the same potential for good and evil.

However, in my own experiences, I witnessed the atrocities of racism against Black Americans. Prejudice by everyone, but racism by White Americans against Black Americans. I have also seen prejudiced police of all types and colors. Nevertheless, White cops perpetrated the most damaging and dehumanizing acts – because they involved both prejudice 'and' racism.

I have also witnessed many more acts of unprovoked violence 'against' cops than the reverse. Most cops I know are the opposite of racists and genuinely want "to serve and to protect." Police are regularly assaulted just for being police (FBI, Law Enforcement Officers Assaulted, Table 80, 2019), and many, including my partner, get killed (ODMP, 2023). It is not uncommon for police officers to be ambushed, punched, spit upon, kicked, stabbed, injured, paralyzed, and killed.

We never parked our patrol cars near a high-rise building's entrance in our high crime precinct. It would "rain bricks," as we described debris thrown out windows and off rooftops at us. Sometimes, parking away from the main lobby doors was not enough. One officer in our command was hit on the head with a brick and permanently disabled.

WHY I NO LONGER CARRY

We would only order food if we could see it prepared or in plain sight on a warming rack. All too often, our food would be compromised in the back kitchen. I bring this out only to give a small glimpse of the anti-cop sentiments.

This is not an excuse for bad police behavior. Any police abuse is an abomination, but many people focus on just that, not the genuine dangers and risks police face every second of their day. I respond to shootings that involve police officers. The NYC media consistently ignores Black officer shootings and highlights White officer shootings. And most NYPD officers on patrol are minorities (NYPD Demographics, 2013).

Many do not realize that most people shot by police in America are White, and most Blacks are shot by non-White officers (Menifield, 2019). However, White-on-Black shootings sell headlines. Again, this is not to deny racism in policing or the wider society. But it is not as the media often portrays. The media constantly wants to generate profit. Blood, color, and racism sell.

GUNAHOLIC

I bring all the above out for two reasons. The most important is to provide context for why more minorities are arrested per capita in some of the larger cities. The second is to keep my brothers and sisters in blue safe. Rogue cops put the lives of all other officers in peril. They leave lousy blood in community/police relationships. A police officer can make multiple arrests and not remember names or faces. However, civilians arrested without discretion will never forget that negative police experience. They do not have to know precisely why they were not given a break or let go. They just knew something was not fair and did not feel right.

My partner left a wife and two young twin daughters behind when he was killed. His felony murderers intentionally set out that night to kill a cop. The group's ringleader testified in court that cops mistreated him, so he was paying back those wrongs. He made a bad choice and got one of the many good ones. When my partner was not on patrol, he was a beloved and gregarious pastor at a church in Central Harlem.

Another consideration is car or pedestrian stops. Police are much more interested in your hands than the color of your face. When police stopped anyone in the high-crime areas where I worked, we almost always assumed a gun was involved. The preponderance of guns increases tensions within the community. Many believe that minorities are treated differently from Whites when stopped by police. In some cases, I am sure they are correct. However, do not assume Whites are given a pass when pulled over or stopped in the neighborhood.

When I get stopped on the road, I pull over, turn off my engine, open all windows, and put my hands outside for the officer to see. If my family is in the car, we all show our hands. That's how I was trained in the 1980s South Bronx, and I have not deviated since.

Every day, well over 100 police officers are assaulted (FBI, Law Enforcement Officers Assaulted, Table 80, 2019). Cops don't feel safe just because the person they are stopping is White. I have also been involved in several police ambush-style killings. Moreover, I became familiar with policing in other nations. Where guns are uncommon, police/community interactions are much less defensive. In some countries, police only sometimes request to see your hands. When I first learned about this, I was surprised. They assume you are not armed in those nations. That is the opposite of here.

Most cops enjoy their jobs and truly like the people they serve, regardless of color. Interracial marriages between cops and community members (like my marriage) are common. Today's rise in discrimination against police makes it worse for everyone. Racism and discrimination are not solely the responsibility of the police or the community. We can only fix racism and hatred if we stop regarding people of any color or profession as the "other."

Let's not be distracted by other people's prejudices. For every prejudiced or racist cop, there is a discriminatory or racist member of the community, and vice versa. That does not excuse anyone, but let's focus on this urgent gun problem. All colors kill, and all colors get killed. We all bleed the same red color and are all brothers and sisters in this one human family. We can fix this by working together, not by finger-pointing. We cannot ignore or cover up the relevant causes and issues related to structural racism, but let's fix this together.

WHY I NO LONGER CARRY

I digressed, but this perspective must be understood outside of law enforcement. I may have offended some, but I am only sharing my personal experiences subject to my limitations and biases. The main topic and this digression have in common that being Black is not a cause of crime. Poverty and other social and economic factors influence crime, not color. Even if all Black gun violence is deleted from the totals, the US still leads the developed world in gun violence, murder, and suicide (Gramlich, 2023) (Grinshteyn, 2019) (Hemenway & Miller, 2000).

GUNAHOLIC

BULLET POINT 16

ARE THERE REASONS TO CARRY?

In Some Circumstances, But at Great Risk

As described in previous sections, legal guns in the hands of civilians are rarely fired in self-defense (Hemenway D, 2015). I've carried firearms professionally and as a civilian in high-crime neighborhoods. I want to share something that is not well-known outside of law enforcement:

Police officers sometimes unchamber ('unload') their pistols when working alone in dangerous environments. In NYC, this is referred to by some cops as "project carry," "subway carry," or "elevator carry." This is not common or official practice, but it remains an option for officers in perilous places. Pistols are grabbed and stolen from police more than many realize. Even in relatively safe environments, police are subjected to sudden and unprovoked attacks (Homeland Security, 2021). Many are shot, injured, paralyzed, or killed with their police service pistols.

The NYPD Police Academy taught us that "Every run is a gun run." (A 'run' is when police are called to respond.) Every run is a 'gun run' because at least one weapon is always involved – the officer's gun. Armed civilians should understand the significance of this police training. The officer may be doing everything by the book, with years of experience, but no officer can read the mind of someone just walking by or standing next to them in an elevator.

Corrections officers similarly do not enter prisoner areas with their firearms. It is against regulations. They store them in gun lockers for the same reason police officers sometimes unload their pistols. Corrections and police officers in high-risk environments don't want to increase the chance of their guns being turned against them.

Working as a civilian in similar high-crime areas, I often took the same precautions. I would rarely enter an elevator in a high crime building or a crowded subway with my pistol ready-loaded. There are safer ways to defend yourself, but those are outside the scope of this book.

Many armed civilians I know seem troubled to leave their homes without a gun. I think that sometimes concerns insecurity, fear, and intimidation. However, I am not a psychologist, so I will not elaborate. That would also detract from the main point. Regardless, I do not think it should be legal for most people to carry a fully loaded weapon in public.

What if you shoot someone? Realize you may save your life, but another life is taken. That may sound like just collateral damage, but in real life, using deadly force affects you mentally and psychologically. Only a few authors today touch on this aspect of shootings (Finch, 2015). It also involves not just the shooter and victim. It affects the hospital trauma team, family, friends, and the local community.

Even physically, your hearing is affected when you fire a gun, especially indoors (Chen, 2011) (Hall-Gale, 2014). Police routinely are hospitalized after shootings to be evaluated and treated for tinnitus (ringing and potential hearing loss) (Stewart, 2023) and trauma. You go right to the hospital after a shooting incident. I have never seen a cop not hospitalized after a shooting. I always have the option of meeting them at the hospital if I arrive late at the crime scene.

You're not off the hook if you escape a self-defense situation with no injuries. You will almost invariably find yourself in litigation. Civilians too, are almost always involved in litigation after the use of firearms. Even brandishing a gun may result in legal action. Some are ruined financially after using a weapon, even in cases of justifiable self-defense. Moreover, after taking armed action, your residence and your family can quickly become a target of retribution. Add that to the many other risks of using a firearm.

WHY I NO LONGER CARRY

Police officers are aware of the legal implications of firing a gun. After most NYPD shootings I am familiar with, there was litigation. No matter how professional the officer may have acted, defense attorneys advise their arrestees to issue civilian complaints against the officers, and then the more serious litigation commences.

That is one reason most NYPD civilian complaints are unsubstantiated. There are about one hundred filed every week. In NYPD nomenclature, most are not sustained, unfounded, or exonerated (ACLU, 2023) (NYPD CCRB, 2023). This does not deny wrongdoing, but complaints and litigation are almost guaranteed after arrests and shootings, regardless of the facts.

As an armed citizen, you may save a life, but chances are you will fare much better without a gun. Realize that you and your loved ones are in great danger when you pull out a firearm. Think of it like a police officer taking their child to a crime. A caring parent will not do that, but if the same officer pulls a gun in a family restaurant, it's little different from taking the child to a crime scene. If the weapon is fired, the child's hearing can be damaged, and it will be forever traumatized. Or worse, the child can be shot by friendly fire or by the criminals. You don't know if the armed perpetrator is acting alone or with accomplices.

Much more can be said about the risks of carrying. The most important thing to realize is that a gun is more often a liability than an asset. While anything is possible, and you may one day need a weapon, there is a greater chance you will regret ever owning one, and your life and the lives of your loved ones will be turned forever upside down.

Even if you need a weapon, there are better and less risky weapons than firearms. That is a topic that lies beyond the scope of this book. Nevertheless, even giant grizzly bears are often better thwarted with bear spray, and with less injury to humans, than with firearms (Smith, 2010).

Some may have more of a need to carry firearms, especially those in dangerous environments and where access to law enforcement is limited. Sometimes, retired police officers must remain wary of job-related threats to themselves and their families. They are also professionally trained and have practical experience with firearms. Some without such training and experience may also have a particular need for arms. However, that is not an excuse for arming the public. The Second Amendment does not grant us "a right to keep and carry any weapon whatsoever in any manner whatsoever and for whatever purpose." (U.S. Supreme Court, 2008).

GUNAHOLIC

BULLET POINT 17

ARE GUNS THE CORE PROBLEM?

A Personal Reflection

If we didn't invent firearms, we'd invent other things to kill with. So no, guns are not the core problem. I believe disunity is the core problem, complicated in America by guns.

GUNAHOLIC

We don't give dangerous things to kids to play with. As every parent knows, children can find other ways to hurt themselves. That doesn't make parents less vigilant. They still do their best to prevent their children from playing with known hazardous objects like knives and matches. As children grow into adolescents, they become increasingly rebellious. They are more independent and unruly but require support, guidance, and assistance.

You can say America (and the world) is at this rebellious and overly independent adolescent stage of development. We must strictly curtail virtually unlimited firearms until we get past this competitive adolescent stage. Despite numerous half-baked gun laws made with even the best intentions, we can see how little they do to prevent gun violence.

When we mature into adulthood, we will realize we're part of a larger community and, ultimately, the human family. We will recognize more of what we have in common and work better together. We will increasingly sacrifice our needs for others, including those we do not know and even our enemies. We will see past imperfections in others and realize we have equal or even more significant flaws. We will focus on our essence as human beings. This will signify the maturity of human and social development.

Racism is one major hurdle we must still overcome. Prejudice does not belong to any group, color, religion, orientation, or political affiliation. However, 'racism' per se is dehumanizing and is usually associated with power. Different groups in other parts of the world are in control and are the dominant racists. We are all equally human; therefore, we share the same potential for good and evil regardless of what part of the world we live in or what we look like.

We're all members of one human family. Whether we follow the teachings of Krishna, Moses, Buddha, Christ, Muhammad, or Baha'u'llah, we are taught the same lessons of love, less the changing historical traditions that we sadly still fight over. Some refer to their higher power by no name, and that is fine, too, since none of us understand that realm anyway. Regardless of label or not, we must unite on the core principles of religion and human morals.

GUNAHOLIC

Comprehensive and multi-faceted gun reform is today's abolition movement. We cannot settle for piecemeal gun regulations, no matter how many get enacted into law. We must unite like our ancestors of all colors did and not settle for "gradual emancipation" from gun slavery. Comprehensive gun reform is the only practical solution currently available to stop the immediate and continuous flow of blood in our homes, streets, cities, parks, shopping malls, theatres, places of worship, universities, high schools, elementary schools, and daycares.

Despite my gun addiction, I finally decided to kick the habit. Faith was necessary to gain the strength to make that final jump. However, my daily motivation was the constant news stream about gun violence across America and attendance at too many police funerals.

I hope you found helpful information about gun violence and control in this book. Moreover, if you or anyone you know are or were victims of gun violence, please accept my sincere condolences.

WHY I NO LONGER CARRY

BULLET POINT 18

ACTION PLAN

Simple Steps That Make a Difference

1. CONNECT:

The root cause of gun violence and many other challenges is disunity. The first and most important thing we can all do is to reach out to people and connect. This is more profound and effective at making a safer world than many realize. If you are the type to read this, you already know that.

2. EXPAND YOUR CIRCLE:

The more effort it takes to connect to some people or groups, the more critical it is to bridge those divides. Our strength is not our diversity but our unity in diversity. Make connections starting with those around you and expand the circle.

3. DISCUSS GUN CONTROL

Now that you have connected with more people, share your wisdom about gun control (and other important issues). Remain open to learning from others. Consult, work together, review your progress, and adapt as necessary.

Listed below are a few gun control organizations that I recommend. You may find them helpful. Some get partisan, some are affiliated with others, and some do not focus specifically on gun violence. There are local and other groups not listed that also do excellent work. Search for gun control organizations or advocacy groups that best fit your style and get involved as you can.

WHY I NO LONGER CARRY

Brady
Brady United; United Against Gun Violence
https://www.bradyunited.org

Everytown
Everytown for Gun Safety; Everytown for Gun Safety Action Fund
https://www.everytown.org

Giffords
Giffords Law Center
https://giffords.org

Moms Demand Action
https://momsdemandaction.org

Pew Research Center
https://www.pewresearch.org

Red, Blue, and Brady (Excellent Podcast Series)
https://www.bradyunited.org/podcast

Sandy Hook Promise

https://www.sandyhookpromise.org

The Trace

https://www.thetrace.org

Violence Policy Center

https://vpc.org

WHY I NO LONGER CARRY

POSTSCRIPT

From Another Angle

I write this section as an independent postscript. It is only from my personal experiences. I hesitated to include this since it's slightly off-subject. However, I think it indirectly relates to gun violence. I hope you appreciate this:

Many animals evolved with defensive features like venom or claws. We would all be biologically armed if evolution required a lethal body part. Instead, we developed not just brains that all animals have but something only humans have – our 'mind.' This essentially is our defense. Our mind includes self-consciousness, the ability to ponder, reflect, pray, and even invent.

A brain can be damaged at birth, compromised with a disability, or weakened later in life. Regardless of physical or mental brain issues a child or adult may suffer, they still have 100% of a human 'mind.' Our mind functions apart from the brain and is not the same thing.

Someone can have both arms and legs amputated and even have parts of their brain removed in neurosurgery, but their 'mind' is not reduced. The mind, or center of consciousness, is sometimes more aware when it is not hindered by everyday physical or cognitive brain functioning. That person often achieves greatness from such intense suffering.

An example is the dream. After we dream of running, we wake up and may remember that dream. However, our brain was not coordinating movements with our legs and feet. We did not run out of bed. The same is true when we meditate. We go places with our thoughts without the brain coordinating motion. We're even taught to nominally 'turn off' our brain during meditation.

Animals can not reflect. They cannot plan their lives. Animals will never invent rockets and travel to outer space. They are captives of the world of nature and cannot rise above it. Some animals have more keen senses than humans. Many see better, especially at night. Many hear better, feel things imperceptible to humans, and smell things we cannot. Some animals have sharper memories than we do. They can find their way back home from miles away. A friend's dog or cat will remember you, even after not seeing you for some time. How quickly we forget even people's names and faces.

The reason we are 'smarter' than all animals is not due to the cognitive functioning of our brains concerning our senses, which many animals have at greater capacity. Our brilliance comes not from our physical brain or the information we absorb from studying.

Our brilliance comes from that unseen common-sense awareness or consciousness – our human mind. Some very learned people need more understanding of the world around them. And some unschooled people are much wiser and more aware. Human wisdom and learning combined are the best of both, and we should strive to achieve not just wisdom but learning and knowledge.

Cognitively disabled children or adults can outshine others with this unique aspect of the mind. Artificial intelligence (AI) is much 'smarter' than we are in ways (like some animals) but will never surpass human 'wisdom.' AI is the result of our ability to invent it. AI did not create itself – the human mind and our power of discovery did. AI can mimic the human brain but not the human mind.

I write this from experience after being pronounced dead when my brain was crushed and lost blood flow. Even to medical experts, I was presumed dead and put in the morgue. My family went to the morgue to identify me. The local radio news reported that I was killed. However, my 'mind' never failed. It became stronger during that trying time. I still recall my awareness, as fellow cops and medical experts thought I was dead along with my unfortunate police partner.

When I see people with intellectual or cognitive disabilities, I do not regard them as 'incomplete.'

WHY I NO LONGER CARRY

This is not to deny their genuine challenges. I understand it is a tremendous burden for them and their families. Nevertheless, I know that their 'minds' are equal to or greater than many. They are not victims, per se, but survivors.

I suspect many challenges are put before us to assist us, not harm us. We grow from pain and suffering. Unfortunately, we recognize many of the benefits later. I am just beginning to appreciate some of my own. Much of our growth from today's suffering will be apparent in the next realm. In the meantime, our 'minds' continue to grow forever, even as our 'brains' will one day become dust and nothing more.

I write this as a personal reflection to underscore that we already have the best weapon to defend ourselves with – the powerful and mysterious human 'mind.' The relevant point concerning gun violence is this: If evolution deemed it necessary for humans to be physically armed, we would have weapons like venom or claws. However, our greatest and most potent weapon is the human mind.

GUNAHOLIC

If we arm ourselves with our minds, we can best protect "ourselves and our Posterity," as our Constitution upholds.

That is why I no longer carry.

WHY I NO LONGER CARRY

ABOUT THE AUTHOR

& FINAL THOUGHTS

I am a retired police officer, a member of a police trauma team that responds to NYPD shootings and suicides, and a business owner in the NYC commercial construction industry. I sometimes teach graduate business as a part-time adjunct professor. I am not an academic, but I studied research methodology and statistics at universities in the USA and Switzerland, undergraduate and graduate. That gave me a foundation to understand research papers from both gun rights and gun control advocates.

During a high-speed police chase in 1988, my partner was killed, and I was seriously injured and pronounced dead while pursuing armed felons (Terry, 1988). After five felons committed an armed robbery, they had a gunfight with the first two responding officers. Several then stole their police car.

When the two officers called for assistance, we attempted to stop the stolen police car. Two felons fired out the broken back window aiming at the police cars in pursuit. As the felons ran out of ammo, they tossed used guns out the window and kept firing new ones. (This was before easy pistol magazine changes. They were left with just one revolver in the end.)

My partner and I tried to speed to the front of them to avoid being shot. Our police car got knocked into a post at full speed and exploded upon impact. It's on the front cover of this book. My partner was ejected far from the car and died immediately. I was trapped inside our burning patrol car and pronounced dead from multiple injuries, including burns, broken backbones, and a crushed head. Broken glass was embedded in my flesh for months (Police Chase Aftermath: Bronx, June, 1988).

I learned of my partner's death after waking up in the morgue. My partner and I patrolled the South Bronx at the height of the crack epidemic when there were five murders for every murder today (NYPD, 2023). Despite the dangers, I felt invincible with my guns – until he was killed. Though we crashed and the gunfire did not directly kill my partner, the illegal handguns fired sent me on a journey from trusting guns with my life to blaming them for his and countless deaths.

After recovering from my injuries, I eventually returned to 'serve and protect' in the housing projects in the same Police Service Area #7 in the South Bronx (NYPD South Bronx Precinct, 2023). I later accepted the police department's previous offer of accident disability and retired.

My wife did not want my police firearms kept at home since I was now retired and no longer on patrol. I grew up associating guns with protection, but she grew up in a high-crime neighborhood and associated them with murder. However, we both agreed on the risks that guns pose to kids.

When our children got older, I began carrying firearms again. However, my ambivalence about firearms quickly returned as gun deaths and mass shootings increased. I was appalled by the false mantras spread by gun rights advocates, many of whom, including NRA representatives, despise the government, ATF, DOJ, FBI, and police. (They despise the United Nations too. Anything that represents law and order in our world and compromises any hint of personal freedom.) Many police officers are unaware of smears made against law enforcement by NRA members and extreme-right gun owners (Mak, 2021). They proudly display NRA stickers on their cars – I no longer do since I regard the NRA as increasingly anti-government and law enforcement.

From patrolling in the 1980s to my current work on an NYPD trauma response team, I have never encountered a legal gun owner 'ever' firing a gun in self-defense. As referenced in this book, surveys support these observations that civilians rarely fire firearms in self-defense.

As gun violence increased despite claims that guns protect us, I could no longer personally justify carrying a lethal weapon every day. I was significantly influenced by seemingly endless news of gun violence and mass shootings (McGraw, 2021). I felt I was participating in our fatally irresponsible gun culture by carrying my pistol

WHY I NO LONGER CARRY

without ample need. Regardless, I do not judge those with a valid reason to carry.

I feel no less protected today and am freer than ever. I do not worry about the dangers of carrying a lethal weapon as I once did. I don't worry about a family member being shot as I take defensive action. Armed criminals often shoot back and hit bystanders, including children. I don't even worry about what to wear to conceal my pistol. And I don't worry about someone grabbing my gun and using it against me or others.

Ultimately, I don't have to be constantly aware of my weapon. When carrying a deadly weapon, your entire worldview changes. You endlessly look at others as potential threats and always look around suspiciously. You see the world and people in a negative light. When you carry a lethal weapon, you must always be vigilant. You are taught to be 100% aware of your firearm and surroundings. Think about that. Your entire center of awareness is a firearm and potential violence. That alone impacts your worldview. Today, I look at people as people, not as potential threats. This is more liberating than I can adequately describe. And that doesn't make me naïve either.

GUNAHOLIC

Survivors of gun violence often suffer from PTSD, anxiety, and depression. The trauma of gun violence has a ripple effect on families, hospitals, and communities, causing fear, grief, and loss. My wife and children experienced some of the ripples from my gun-related trauma.

I feel we need to acknowledge the root causes of gun violence. Poverty, hatred, and prejudice all contribute to gun violence. Nevertheless, it is ultimately a result of disunity. We must create a society that values all human life over conflicting individual views about "freedom."

As a retired police officer and lifelong gun owner, I have seen firsthand what guns can do to us. It is time to have more serious conversations about firearms' dangers, liabilities, and risks rather than endlessly debating the Second Amendment and gun parts.

Thank you for reading, Chip Plunkett
Chiplunkett@gmail.com (note: one p)

WORKS CITED

109th Congress. (2005, October 26). *Protection of Lawful Commerce in Arms Act.* Retrieved from Congress.gov: https://www.congress.gov/bill/109th-congress/senate-bill/397/text

ACLU. (2023). *NYPD MISCONDUCT COMPLAINT DATABASE.* Retrieved from ACLU of New York: https://www.nyclu.org/en/campaigns/nypd-misconduct-database#:~:text=The%20NYPD%20Misconduct%20Complaint%20Database,complaint%20records%20involving%20107%2C187%20incidents.

American College of Cardiology. (2016, December 5). *Even Moderate, Habitual Alcohol Consumption Can Cause Irregular Heartbeat.* Retrieved 2023, from https://www.acc.org/about-acc/press-releases/2016/12/05/14/06/even-moderate-habitual-alcohol-consumption-can-cause-irregular-heartbeat

Anglemyer, A. P. (2014, January 21). The Accessibility of Firearms and Risk for Suicide and Homicide Victimization Among Household Members. *Annals of Internal Medicine.*

Associated Press. (2022, October 10). Mexico Files 2nd Lawsuit Against Arms Dealers in US. *US News & World Report.*

ATF. (2021). *ANNUAL FIREARMS MANUFACTURING AND EXPORT REPORT.* Retrieved 2023, from Bureau of Alcohol, Tobacco, Firearms and Explosives: https://www.atf.gov/explosives/docs/report/afmer2021finalwebreportpdf/download

ATF. (2023). *Crime Guns Recovered and Traced Within the United States and Its Territories.* Retrieved 2023, from National Firearms Commerce and Trafficking Assessment (NFCTA): Crime Guns - Volume Two: https://www.atf.gov/firearms/docs/report/nfcta-volume-ii-part-iii-crime-guns-recovered-and-traced-us/download

ATF. (2023). *Federal Firearms Licensee Theft/Loss Report - 2021.* Retrieved from Bureau of Alcohol, Tobacco, Firearms and

Explosives: https://www.atf.gov/resource-center/federal-firearms-licensee-theftloss-report-2021

ATF. (2023). *Gun Control Act of 1968.* Retrieved from Bureau of Alcohol, Tobacco, Firearms and Explosives: https://www.atf.gov/rules-and-regulations/gun-control-act

Atwood, J. E. (2012). *America and Its Guns: A Theological Exposé.* Cascade books.

Austin, M. (2013). *That's Not What They Meant About Guns!* Prometheus Books.

Bai, M. (2001, March 1). The Gun Crowd's Guru. *Newsweek.*

Bailey, C. (2017, October 4). *More Americans Killed by Guns Since 1968 Than in All U.S. Wars — Combined.* Retrieved from NBC News: https://www.nbcnews.com/storyline/las-vegas-shooting/more-americans-killed-guns-1968-all-u-s-wars-combined-n807156

Barrigar, C. (2023, May 30). Luke 22:36 and Hsiao's Libertarian 'Theology' of Gun Ownership. *Evangelical Quarterly: An International Review of Bible and Theology, 94*(2), 133-153.

Bartlett, C. S., & Helfet, D. L. (2000, January 8). Ballistics and Gunshot Wounds: Effects on

Musculoskeletal Tissues. *Journal of the American Academy of Orthopaedic Surgeons, 1*, 21-36.

Barton, C. (2023, April 27). *Lawmakers Push for Guns to be Regulated Like Other Products*. Retrieved from The Trace: https://www.thetrace.org/2023/04/congress-gun-safety-bills-cpsc-sig-sauer/#:~:text=Guns%20are%20one%20of%20the,models%20found%20to%20be%20defective.

Bhatt, J. L. (2017, October). Epidemiology of firearm and other noise exposures in the United States. *Laryngoscope, 127*(10), E340-E346.

Borgogna, N. C. (2022). The precarious masculinity of firearm ownership. *Psychology of Men & Masculinities, 23*(2), 173–182.

Braga AA, C. P. (2018, July 27). The Association of Firearm Caliber With Likelihood of Death From Gunshot Injury in Criminal Assaults. *JAMA Nework Open, 1*(3).

Braga, A. A. (2021). Firearm Instrumentality: Do Guns Make Violent Situations More Lethal? *Review of Criminology, 4*(1), 147-164.

Braga, A. B. (2021, October). Underground Gun Markets and the Flow of Illegal Guns into the Bronx and Brooklyn: A Mixed Methods Analysis. *Journal of Urban Health, 98*, 596–608.

Brucato, G. (2021). *Psychotic symptoms in mass shootings v. mass murders not involving firearms: findings from the Columbia mass murder database.* Retrieved from Columbia University Department of Psychiatry: https://www.columbiapsychiatry.org/sites/default/files/media/documents/2021-02/psychotic-symptoms-in-mass-shootings-v-mass-murders-not-involving-firearms-findings-from-the-columbia-mass-murder-database.pdf

Busse, R. (2021). *Gunfight: My Battle Against the Industry that Radicalized America.* PublicAffairs.

Carr, B. G. (2010, September-October). A review of legislation restricting the intersection of firearms and alcohol in the U.S. *Public Health Reports, 125*(5), 674–679.

Carter, P. M. (2022, March). Firearm ownership, attitudes, and safe storage practices among a nationally representative sample of older

U.S. adults age 50 to 80. *Preventive Medicine, 156*(106955).

Cassandra K. Crifasi, P. M. (2018, April). Storage Practices of US Gun Owners in 2016. *AJPH Research, 108*(4). Retrieved from AJPH: https://ajph.aphapublications.org/doi/pdf/10.2105/AJPH.2017.304262

CDC. (2021, March 31). *Sleep Inertia*. Retrieved from NIOSH Training for Nurses on Shift Work and Long Work Hours: https://www.cdc.gov/niosh/work-hour-training-for-nurses/longhours/mod7/03.html#:~:text=Sleep%20inertia%20is%20a%20temporary,mood%20after%20awakening%20from%20sleep.

CDC. (2023). *Alcohol and Cancer.* Retrieved from CDC.gov: https://www.cdc.gov/cancer/alcohol/index.htm

CDC Firearm Mortality. (2023). *Firearm Mortality by State.* Retrieved from CDC: https://www.cdc.gov/nchs/pressroom/sosmap/firearm_mortality/firearm.htm

Chang, S. (2018). *Our National Psychosis: Guns, Terror, and Hegemonic Masculinity.* Retrieved from Harvard CRCL Law

Review: https://harvardcrcl.org/wp-content/uploads/sites/10/2018/11/Chang.pdf

Chen, L. M. (2011, September). *CDC Noise and Lead Exposures at an Outdoor Firing Range — California.* Retrieved from Workplace Safety and Health: https://www.cdc.gov/niosh/hhe/reports/pdfs/2011-0069-3140.pdf

Chmielewski, K. R. (2023, July 30). *Mass Shooting.* Retrieved from Britannica: https://www.britannica.com/topic/mass-shooting

Cimons, M. (2023, March 31). No, moderate drinking isn't good for your health. *Washington Post.*

Colajuta, J. (2022). *The NRA and the American Gun Control Debate The Original Intent of the Second Amendment and the Wrong Meaning of the Right to Bear Arms.* Vincenzo Nappi.

Congress.gov. (2005, October 26). *S.397 - Protection of Lawful Commerce in Arms Act.* Retrieved from 109th Congress: https://www.congress.gov/bill/109th-congress/senate-bill/397/text

Constitution.gov. (2013). *ArtI.S8.C18.1 Overview of Necessary and Proper Clause.* Retrieved

2023, from Constitution Annotated: Analysis and Interpretation of the U.S. Constutution: https://constitution.congress.gov/browse/essay/artI-S8-C18-1/ALDE_00001242/

Cooter, A. (2022). US Domestic Militias' Intersections with Government and Authority: How a Sociology of Individualism Informs Their Praxis. In D. L.-K. Neubert, *Local Self-Governance and Varieties of Statehood. Contributions to Political Science.* Springer, Cham.

Cornell, S. (2008). *A Well-Regulated Militia: The Founding Fathers and the Origins of Gun Control in America.* Oxford University Press.

CPSC. (2023). *USCPSC*. Retrieved from Consumer Product Safety Commission: https://www.cpsc.gov

Crifasi CK, P. K. (2016, December). Assaults against U.S. law enforcement officers in the line-of-duty: situational context and predictors of lethality. *Injury Epidemiology, 3(1)*(29).

Cukier, W. (2002, August 12). More guns, more death, Medicine, Conflict and Survival.

Medicine, Conflict and Survival, 18(4), 367-379.

DeBrabander, F. (2015). *Do Guns Make Us Free?: Democracy and the Armed Society.* Yale University Press.

Department of Justice. (2023). *Living arrangements of children by race/ethnicity, 1970-2022.* Retrieved 2023, from Office of Juvenile Justice and Delinquency Prevention: https://www.ojjdp.gov/ojstatbb/population/qa01202.asp?qaDate=2022#:~:text=Between%20201970%20and%202022%2C%20the,to%2045.6%25%20for%20Black%20youth.

Detty, M. (2013). *Guns Across the Border: How and Why the U.S. Government Smuggled Guns into Mexico: The Inside Story.* Skyhorse.

Diaz, T. (2013). *The Last Gun: How Changes in the Gun Industry Are Killing Americans and What It Will Take to Stop It.* The New Press.

Donohue, J. J. (2022). The Effect of Permissive Gun Laws on Crime. *The ANNALS of the American Academy of Political and Social Science, 704*(1), 92–117.

Donohue, J. J. (2022, June). Why Does Right-to-Carry Cause Violent Crime to Increase?

Stanford Law School; National Bureau of Economic Research.

Dowdell, E. B. (2022, July-August). *School Shooters: Patterns of Adverse Childhood Experiences, Bullying, and Social Media.* Retrieved from Journal of Pediatric Healthcare: https://www.sciencedirect.com/science/article/abs/pii/S089152452100290X

Duchesne J, T. S. (2022, April 1). State Gun Law Grades and Impact on Mass Shooting Event Incidence: An 8-Year Analysis. *Journal of American College of Surgeons, 234*(4), 645-651.

Dutton, D. G. (2013, September-October 5). Paranoid thinking in mass shooters. *Agression and Violent Behavior, 18*(5), 548-553.

Eckholm, E. (2015, December 8). How an effort to close loopholes in California's assault weapons law was thwarted. *The New York Times.*

FBI. (2019). *Arrests by Race and Ethnicity Table 43.* Retrieved from Crime in the United States 2019: https://ucr.fbi.gov/crime-in-the-u.s/2019/crime-in-the-u.s.-2019/tables/table-43

FBI. (2019). *Expanded Homicide Data Table 6.* Retrieved 2023, from FBI UCR 2019: https://ucr.fbi.gov/crime-in-the-u.s/2019/crime-in-the-u.s.-2019/tables/expanded-homicide-data-table-6.xls

FBI. (2019). *Expanded Homicide Data Table 8.* Retrieved from Crime in the US: https://ucr.fbi.gov/crime-in-the-u.s/2019/crime-in-the-u.s.-2019/tables/expanded-homicide-data-table-8.xls

FBI. (2019). *Law Enforcement Officers Assaulted, Table 80.* Retrieved from FBI UCR: https://ucr.fbi.gov/leoka/2019/topic-pages/tables/table-80.xls

FBI UCR Chicago. (2023). *Summary Crime Reported by the Chicago Police Department 1985-2021.* Retrieved from FBI Crime Data Explorer: https://cde.ucr.cjis.gov/LATEST/webapp/#/pages/explorer/crime/crime-trend

FBI UCR NYC. (2023). *New York City Police Department.* Retrieved from FBI Crime Data Explorer: https://cde.ucr.cjis.gov/LATEST/webapp/#/pages/explorer/crime/crime-trend

Finances Online. (2023). *45 Single Parent Statistics You Can't Ignore: 2023 Gender, Race & Challenges.* Retrieved 2023, from Finances Online: https://financesonline.com/single-parent-statistics/

Finch, L. (2015). *Female and Armed: A Woman's Guide to Advanced Situational Awareness, Concealed Carry, and Defensive Shooting Techniques.* Skyhorse.

Franks, M. A. (2019). *The Cult of the Constitution: Our Deadly Devotion to Guns and Free Speech.* Stanford University Press.

Garfinkel, R. (2018, March 26). *America's Gun Addiction.* Retrieved from Psychology Today: https://www.psychologytoday.com/us/blog/time-out/201803/americas-gun-addiction#:~:text=The%20brain%20is%20flooded%20with,and%20with%20other%20enjoyable%20activities.

Giffords. (2023). *Gun Industry Immunity.* Retrieved from GIffords Law Center to Prevent Gun Violence: https://giffords.org/lawcenter/gun-laws/policy-areas/other-laws-policies/gun-industry-immunity/

Giffords. (2023). *Gun Shows.* Retrieved from Giffords Law Center for Gun Violence: https://giffords.org/lawcenter/gun-laws/policy-areas/gun-sales/gun-shows/#:~:text=Often%20held%20at%20public%20venues,the%20United%20States%20each%20year.

Giles, K. (2021). *Jesus Unarmed: How the Prince of Peace Disarms Our Violence.* Quoir.

Gilles, S. G. (2013, Fall). *Insurance as Gun Control; A Liability Insurance Mandate for Firearm Owners May Pass Constitutional Muster, But Its Effect on Violent Crime Would Be Modest.* Retrieved from Heinonline: https://heinonline.org/HOL/LandingPage?handle=hein.journals/rcatorbg36&div=28&id=&page=

Glock. (2023). *Our SAFE ACTION® System: Always Safe and Always Ready.* Retrieved July 2023, from Glock Perfection: https://us.glock.com/en/learn/glock-pistols/safe-action-system

Government Accountability Office. (2021, February 22). *Firearms Trafficking: U.S. Efforts to Disrupt Gun Smuggling into Mexico Would Benefit from Additional Data and Analysis.* Retrieved July 2023, from GOA: https://www.gao.gov/products/gao-21-322

Gramlich, J. (2023, April 26). *What the data says about gun deaths in the U.S.* Retrieved from Pew Research Center: https://www.pewresearch.org/short-reads/2023/04/26/what-the-data-says-about-gun-deaths-in-the-u-s/

Grillo, I. (2021). *Blood Gun Money: How America Arms Gangs and Cartels.* Bloomsbury Publishing.

Grinshteyn, E. H. (2019, June). Violent death rates in the US compared to those of the other high-income countries, 2015. *Preventive Medicine, 123*, 20-26.

Gullion, C. L. (2022). Homicide Hot Spots in Chicago: Examining Spatiotemporal Patterns Longitudinally Across Police Beats. *Crime & Delinquency, 0*(0).

Gun Violence Research. (2023). *UNETHICAL BEHAVIOR: John Lott's Missing Survey on Defensive Gun Use.* Retrieved July 2023, from Facts About Firearm Policy Initiative: https://www.gvpedia.org/gun-myths/missing-survey/

Hall-Gale, J. F. (2014, January 1). Pulling the Trigger on Pollution or Jumping the Gun on Gun Control?: An Overview of the Environmental Impacts of Guns and Ammunition. *Environmental Law Journal, 25*(1).

Hals, T. (2022, May 22). Explainer: Can U.S. gunmakers be liable for mass shootings? *Reuters*.

Hannon, L. a. (2005). Violent Crime in African American and White Neighborhoods: Is Poverty's Detrimental Effect Race-Specific? *Journal of Poverty, 9*(3), 49-67.

Hargis, C. (2019, September 19). *Discredited pro-gun researcher John Lott falls apart when you press him.* Retrieved 2023, from Media Matters: https://www.mediamatters.org/john-lott/discredited-pro-gun-researcher-john-lott-falls-apart-when-you-press-him

Hemenway D, S. S. (2015). The epidemiology of self-defense gun use: Evidence from the National Crime Victimization Surveys. *Preventive Medicine, 79*, 22-27.

Hemenway, D. A. (2017, April 10). Whose guns are stolen? The epidemiology of Gun theft victims. *Injury Epidemiology, 4*(11).

Hemenway, D. P., & Miller, a. M. (2000, December). Firearm Availability and Homicide Rates across 26 High-Income Countries. *The Journal of Trauma: Injury, Infection, and Critical Care, 49*(6), 985-988.

Henigan, D. A. (2016). *"Guns Don't Kill People, People Kill People": And Other Myths About Guns and Gun Control.* Beacon Press.

Hockmann K, T. S. (2015). Antimony retention and release from drained and waterlogged shooting range soil under field conditions. *Chemosphere, 134*, 536–543.

Hogg, D. H. (2018). *#NeverAgain: A New Generation Draws the Line.* Random House.

Homeland Security. (2021, October 21). *FBI 2020 Data on Law Enforcement Officers Killed & Assaulted.* Retrieved 2023, from Homeland Security Digital Library: https://www.hsdl.org/c/2020-leoka/

Hoskins K, R. P. (2020, March). Applying Behavioral Economics to Enhance Safe Firearm Storage. *Pediatrics, 145*(3).

Isbell, D. R. (2022, February 15). Misconduct and Questionable Research Practices: The Ethics of Quantitative Data Handling and Reporting in Applied Linguistics. *The*

Modern Language Journal , 106(1), 172-195.

Joslyn, M. H.-M. (2017). Emerging Political Identities? Gun Ownership and Voting in Presidential Elections. *Social Science Quarterly, 98*, 382-396.

Kalesan, B. P. (2016, April 30). Firearm legislation and firearm mortality in the USA: a cross-sectional, state-level study. *Lancet, 387*(10030), 1847-1855.

Kaufman EJ, M. C. (2018). State Firearm Laws and Interstate Firearm Deaths From Homicide and Suicide in the United States: A Cross-sectional Analysis of Data by County. *JAMA Intern Med, 178*(5), 692–700.

Keddie, T. (2023). *Second-Amendment Exegesis of Luke 22:35–53: How Conservative Evangelical Bible Scholars Protect Christian Gun Culture.* Retrieved from Academia: https://www.academia.edu/88841146/Second_Amendment_Exegesis_of_Luke_22_35_53_How_Conservative_Evangelical_Bible_Scholars_Protect_Christian_Gun_Culture_2023_

Kellermann AL, S. G. (1998, August). Injuries and deaths due to firearms in the home. J Trauma. *J Trauma, 45*(2), 263-267.

Kimmel, J. &. (2020). A Behavioral Addiction Model of Revenge, Violence, and Gun Abuse. *The Journal of Law, Medicine & Ethics, 48*(4), 172–178.

Klarevas, L. C. (2019, December 1). The Effect of Large-Capacity Magazine Bans on High-Fatality Mass Shootings, 1990–2017. *American Journal of Public Health, 109*(12), 1754-1761.

Kwon, I.-W. G. (2005, April 22). The Effectiveness of Legislation Controlling Gun Usage A Holistic Measure of Gun Control Legislation. *The American Journal of Economics and Sociology, 64*(2), 533-547.

Lacombe, M. J. (2021). *Firepower: How the NRA Turned Gun Owners into a Political Force.* Princeton University Press.

Lazar, C. (2022). *Summary of The Violence Project: How to Stop a Mass Shooting Epidemic by James Densley & Jillian Peterson Ph.D.*

Lee LK, F. E. (2022). Firearm-Related Injuries and Deaths in Children and Youth. *Pediatrics, 150*(6).

Library of Congress. (2021). *Abraham Lincoln and Emancipation.* Retrieved from Abraham Lincoln Papers at the Library of Congress: https://www.loc.gov/collections/abraham-lincoln-papers/articles-and-essays/abraham-lincoln-and-emancipation/#:~:text=Although%20Lincoln%20personally%20abhorred%20slavery,where%20slavery%20was%20still%20legal.

Library of Congress. (2023). *Abraham Lincoln Papers at the Library of Congress.* Retrieved 2023, from Library of Congress: https://www.loc.gov/collections/abraham-lincoln-papers/articles-and-essays/abraham-lincoln-and-emancipation/timeline/

Lincoln, A. (1863, November 19). *The Gettysburg Address.* (F. Ballard, Ed.) Retrieved 2023, from National Archives: www.nationalarchives.gov/abraham-lincoln

Loesch, D. (2014). *Hands Off My Gun: Defeating the Plot to Disarm America.* Center Street.

Lott, J. R. (2016). *The War on Guns: Arming Yourself Against Gun Control Lies.* Regnery Publishing.

Mak, T. (2021). *Misfire: Inside the Downfall of the NRA*. Dutton.

Martinez, R. (2018). Gun addiction: A public health issue . *Journal of Public Health Management and Practice , 24*(2), 187-189 .

Mascia, J. (2021, January 21). *Discredited Gun Researcher Out at Justice Department.* Retrieved from The Trace: https://www.thetrace.org/2021/01/john-lott-trump-appointee-leave-justice-department-gun-data/

Massachusetts Historical Society. (2013, May). *"This Convulsed Commonwealth": Daniel Shays Attempts to Call a Truce during Shays' Rebellion, the Agrarian Revolt Named for Him.* Retrieved from Massachusetts Historical Society : https://www.masshist.org/object-of-the-month/may-2013

Mauri, A. I. (2019, December). Firearm Storage Practices and Risk Perceptions. *American Journal of Preventive Medicine, 57*(6), 830-835.

McCord, M. B. (2021, June). *PROTESTS, INSURRECTION, AND THE SECOND AMENDMENT: Dispelling the Myth of the Second Amendment.* Retrieved from brennancenter.org: https://www.brennancenter.org/sites/default/files/2021-06/McCord_final_0.pdf

McDougal, T. S. (2013, March). *The Way of the Gun: Estimating Firearms Traffic Across the U.S.-Mexico Border.* Retrieved 2023, from University of San Diego Trans-Border Institute: https://catcher.sandiego.edu/items/peacestudies/way_of_the_gun.pdf

McGraw, S. (2021). *From a Taller Tower: The Rise of the American Mass Shooter.* University of Texas Press.

Meltzer, J. (2014, March). Open Carry for All: Heller and Our Nineteenth-Century Second Amendment. *The Yale Law Journal, 123*(5), 1118-1625.

Menifield, C. E. (2019). *Do white law enforcement officers target minority suspects?* Retrieved from Wiley Online Library: https://onlinelibrary.wiley.com/doi/abs/10.1111/puar.12956

Military. (2023). *Rate of Fire.* Retrieved from Military History Fandom: https://military-history.fandom.com/wiki/Rate_of_fire

Military.com. (2023). *Discovering the Weapons Used in Basic.* Retrieved from Military.com:

https://www.military.com/join-armed-forces/discovering-the-weapons-used-in-basic.html

Miller M, Z. Y. (2022, April 27). Suicide Deaths Among Women in California Living With Handgun Owners vs Those Living With Other Adults in Handgun-Free Homes, 2004-2016. *Journal of the American Medical Association, 79*(6), 582–588.

Mineo, L. (2022, Februay 18). *Stopping toxic flow of guns from U.S. to Mexico.* Retrieved from The Harvard Gazette: https://news.harvard.edu/gazette/story/2022/02/stopping-toxic-flow-of-gun-traffic-from-u-s-to-mexico/

Morgan, R. E. (2022, February). *Criminal Victimization, 2020 – Supplemental Statistical Tables.* Retrieved from U.S. Department of Justice: https://bjs.ojp.gov/content/pub/pdf/cv20sst.pdf

Morland, S. (2023, March 16). Mexico launches appeal in suit against U.S. gun makers. *Reuters.*

Moskos, P. (2008). The Better Part of Valor: Court- Overtime Pay as the Main Determinant for Discretionary Police

Arrests. *Law Enforcement Executive Forum. 8*, pp. 77-94. New York: John Jay College of Criminal Justice.

Moyer, M. W. (2020, April 7). *Will a Gun Keep Your Family Safe? Here's What the Evidence Says.* Retrieved 2023, from The Trace: https://www.thetrace.org/2020/04/gun-safety-research-coronavirus-gun-sales/

Murphey, J. P. (2000, July). *Army Ammunition and Explosives Storage in the United States: 1775-1945.* Retrieved from Camp Stanley Storage Activity: https://www.stanley.army.mil/volume1-6/ICRMP-AppF.pdf

Murphy WJ, T. R. (2007, September). Assessment of Noise Exposure for Indoor and Outdoor Firing Ranges. *Journal of Occupational and Environmental Hygiene, 4*(9), 688-97.

Mustard, D. B. (2000, December). The Impact of Gun Laws on Police Deaths.

Nasheed, J. (2020, July 28). *"Black-on-Black Crime" Is a Dangerous Myth.* Retrieved 2023, from Teen Vogue: https://www.teenvogue.com/story/black-on-black-crime-myth

NCES. (2023). *Indicator 11. Children of Single Parents.* Retrieved from National Center for Education Statistics: https://nces.ed.gov/pubs98/yi/yi11.pdf

NICB. (2022, September 1). *NICB Report Finds Vehicle Thefts Continue to Skyrocket in Many Areas of U.S.* Retrieved from Thefts by State 2019-2021: https://www.nicb.org/news/reports-statistics

NYPD. (2023). *Report Covering the Week 7/17/2023 Through 7/23/2023.* Retrieved from Compstat: https://www.nyc.gov/assets/nypd/downloads/pdf/crime_statistics/cs-en-us-city.pdf

NYPD CCRB. (2023). *Civilian Complaints.* Retrieved from Civilian Complaint Review Board: https://www.nyc.gov/site/ccrb/index.page

NYPD Demographics. (2013). Retrieved from https://app.powerbigov.us/view?r=eyJrIjoiZTI4OTRjZTYtNTYwOC00NzcxLThhYTItOTU5NGNkMzIzYjVlIiwidCI6IjJiOWY1N2ViLTc4ZDEtNDZmYi1iZTgzLWEyYWZkZDdjNjA0MyJ9&pageName=ReportSection

NYPD South Bronx Precinct. (2023). Retrieved from New York City Police Department

PSA 7: https://www.nyc.gov/site/nypd/bureaus/transit-housing/police-service-area-7.page

ODMP. (2023). *Honor Roll of Heroes*. Retrieved from Officer Down Memorial Page: https://www.odmp.org/search/year/2023

O'Toole, M. J.-S. (2022, May 9). *Gun Thefts from Cars: The Largest Source of Stolen Guns.* Retrieved from Everytown for Gun Safety: https://everytownresearch.org/gun-thefts-from-cars-the-largest-source-of-stolen-guns/

Okoronkwo, M. E. (2014, January 1). Of what use is the sword for the disciples of Jesus? A discourse analysis of Luke 22:35-38 in the light of New Testament ethics on non-violence. *Journal for Contextual Hermeneutics in Southern Africa, 113*(1).

Olmstead, M. (2018, February 20). *NYPD Officers Accused of "Collars for Dollars" Arrests at End of Shifts to Rake In Overtime Pay.* Retrieved from Slate: https://slate.com/news-and-politics/2018/02/civil-rights-case-in-new-york-questions-whether-police-officers-make-collars-for-dollars-arrests-for-overtime-pay.html

Pane, L. M. (2018, September 30). As immigrants flow across US border, American guns go south. *Associated Press* .

Parker A. (2019). *For Alison: The Murder of a Young Journalist and a Father's Fight for Gun Safety.* Apollo Publishers.

Parker, K. H. (2017, June 22). *America's Complex Relationship with Guns: The Demographics of Gun Ownership.* Retrieved from Pew Research: https://www.pewresearch.org/social-trends/2017/06/22/the-demographics-of-gun-ownership/

Pason, A. a. (2021). Protesting with guns and conflating the First and Second Amendments: The case of the Bundys. *First Amendment Studies, 55*(2), 102-125.

Pelc C. (2021, November 6). *Moderate alcohol consumption 'should not be recommended for health reasons'.* Retrieved July 2023, from Medical News Today: https://www.medicalnewstoday.com/articles/moderate-alcohol-consumption-should-not-be-recommended-for-health-reasons

Peterson, J. (2021). *The Violence Project: How to Stop a Mass Shooting Epidemic.* Abrams Press.

Philips, J. A. (2002). White, Black, and Latino Homicide Rates: Why the Difference? *Social Problems, 49*(3), 349–373.

Pinholt, E. M. (2014, June 4). "Is There a Gun in the Home?" Assessing the Risks of Gun Ownership in Older Adults. *Journal of the American Geriatrics Society.*

Police Chase Aftermath: Bronx, June. (1988, June 16). Retrieved from Video Vultures: https://www.youtube.com/watch?v=K0TvB6ta3NY

Posess, Z. (2020). A Shot in the Dark: How the Sandy Hook Plaintiffs Established Legal Standing Against the Gun Industry. *Seton Hall Law Review, 51*(2), Article 9.

Powell J L. (2020). *Inside the NRA: A Tell-All Account of Corruption, Greed, and Paranoia within the Most Powerful Political Group in America.* Twelve.

Powell, T. (2016). Gun Lust: An Investigation into America's Sordid Gun Addiction. *International Critical Thought, 6*(1), 119-140.

Rosenthal, E. L. (2019). Guns as addictive stimuli: An examination of personal and contextual influences on compulsive gun use. *Journal of Behavioral Addictions , 8*(4), 566-573.

Salhi C, A. D. (2021). Patterns of gun owner beliefs about firearm risk in relation to firearm storage: a latent class analysis using the 2019 National Firearms Survey. *Injury Prevention, 27*, 271-276.

Sanderson, P. Q. (2018, April 10). Contamination, Fate and Management of Metals in Shooting Range Soils - a Review. *Current Pollution Reports volume, 4*, 175–187.

Schildkraut, J. (2019, March 22). *Assault Weapons, Mass Shootings, and options for Lawmakers.* Retrieved from Rockefeller Institute of Government : https://rockinst.org/wp-content/uploads/2019/03/190321b_Mass-Shootings-and-Assault-Weapons.pdf

Schumann, T. S. (2021). *When Thoughts and Prayers Aren't Enough: A Shooting Survivor's Journey into the Realities of Gun Violence.* IVP.

Semenza, D. (2022, June 21). *More Guns, More Death: The Fundamental Fact that Supports a Comprehensive Approach to Reducing Gun Violence in America.* Retrieved from Rockefeller Institute of Government: https://rockinst.org/blog/more-guns-more-death-the-fundamental-fact-that-supports-a-comprehensive-approach-to-reducing-gun-violence-in-america/

Smith, T. S. (2010, December 10). Efficacy of Bear Deterrent Spray in Alaska. *The Journal of Wildlife Management.*

Smyth, F. (2020). *The NRA: The Unauthorized History.* Flatiron Books.

Solnick, S. H. (2019). Unintentional firearm deaths in the United States 2005–2015. *Injury Epidemiology, 6*(43).

Spangenberg, K. B. (2015, April 27). Firearm Presence in Households of Patients with Alzheimer's Disease and Related Dementias. *Journal of the American Geriatrics Society.*

Spitzer, R. J. (2017). *Gun Law History in the United States and Second Amendment Rights.* Retrieved from Rockefeller Institute of Government: https://scholarship.law.duke.edu/cgi/viewcontent.cgi?article=4825&context=lcp

Statista. (2023). *Motor vehicle theft rate in the United States in 2020, by state (per 100,000 inhabitants).* Retrieved from Statista 2023: https://www.statista.com/statistics/232588/motor-vehicle-theft-rate-in-the-us-by-state/

Statista. (2023). *Number of victims of the worst mass shootings in the United States between*

1982 and July 2023. Retrieved from Statista: https://www.statista.com/statistics/476101/worst-mass-shootings-in-the-us/

Stempel, J. (2021, December 6). Gunmakers not liable for deaths in 2017 Las Vegas shooting massacre, court rules. *Reuters*.

Stephenson, O. W. (1925, January). *The Supply of Gunpowder in 1776*. Retrieved July 2023, from Penelope: https://penelope.uchicago.edu/Thayer/E/Journals/AHR/30/2/Supply_of_Gunpowder_in_1776.html

Stewart, M. P.-A. (2023). *Recreational Firearm Noise Exposure*. Retrieved July 2023, from American Speech-Language-Hearing Association: https://www.asha.org/public/hearing/recreational-firearm-noise-exposure/

Studdert, D. M. (2022, June). Homicide Deaths Among Adult Cohabitants of Handgun Owners in California, 2004 to 2016. *Annals of Internal Medicine*.

Swedler DI, S. M. (2015). Firearm prevalence and homicides of law enforcement officers in the United States. *American Journal of Public Health, 105*, 2042-48.

Tamme, S. (2015, May 14). *Mitigating the Dangers of Ammunition at Fire Incidents.* Retrieved from Fire Engineering: https://www.fireengineering.com/firefighting/mitigating-the-dangers-of-ammunition-at-fire-incidents/#gref

Tatalovich, R. H.-M. (2022). Voting on gun rights: Mapping the electoral scope of the pro-gun constituency in America. *Social Science Quarterly*, 1359–1370.

Terry, D. (1988, June 17). Housing Police Officer Killed in Chase. *New York TImes*, p. B3.

Texas Statutes. (2023). *Tex. Pen. Code § 46.13.* Retrieved from Texas Codes: https://casetext.com/statute/texas-codes/penal-code/title-10-offenses-against-public-health-safety-and-morals/chapter-46-weapons/section-4613-making-a-firearm-accessible-to-a-child

The Trace. (2022, December 9). *How Often Are Guns Involved in Accidental Deaths?* Retrieved 2023, from The Trace: https://www.thetrace.org/2022/12/accidental-shootings-cdc-data-children/

The World Bank - BVI. (2023). *Intentional homicides (per 100,000 people) - British Virgin Islands.* Retrieved from UN Office on Drugs and Crime's International Homicide Statistics database: https://data.worldbank.org/indicator/VC.IHR.PSRC.P5?locations=VG

The World Bank - USVI. (2023). *Intentional homicides (per 100,000 people) - Virgin Islands (U.S.)*. Retrieved from UN Office on Drugs and Crime's International Homicide Statistics database.: https://data.worldbank.org/indicator/VC.IHR.PSRC.P5?locations=VI

Thoreau, R. (2018). *The Right to Bear Arms in a Modern America: The Intent of the Second Amendment and the Right to Keep Arms in a Violent Society.*

Tonetti L, F. M. (2022). Time Course of Motor Sleep Inertia Dissipation According to Age. *Brain Sciences, 12*(4), 424.

Trotta, D. C. (2017, October 2). Two hours of horror, disbelief, as gunman opens fire in Las Vegas. *Reuters*.

Trotti, L. (2017, October). Waking up is the hardest thing I do all day: Sleep inertia and sleep drunkenness. *Sleep Medicines Review, 35*, 76-84.

U.S. Const. amend. II. (n.d.).

U.S. Const. pmbl. (n.d.).

U.S. Drug Enforcement Administration. (2015, July). *United States: Areas of Influence of Major Mexican Transnational Criminal Organizations.* Retrieved 2023, from DEA Intelligence Report: https://www.dea.gov/sites/default/files/2018-07/dir06515.pdf

U.S. Drug Enforcement Administration. (2021, January 28). *Violent drug organizations use human trafficking to expand profits.* Retrieved from US Drug Enforcement Administration: https://www.dea.gov/stories/2021/2021-01/2021-01-28/violent-drug-organizations-use-human-trafficking-expand-profits

U.S. Supreme Court. (2008, June 26). *District of Columbia v. Heller, 2008.* Retrieved from JUSTIA: https://supreme.justia.com/cases/federal/us/554/570/

US Constitution. (2023). *The Constitution of the United States: A Transcription.* Retrieved from https://www.archives.gov/founding-docs/constitution-transcript

USCCA. (2019, December 29). *In Which States Can You Concealed Carry and Drink Alcohol?* Retrieved from US Concealed

Carry Association: https://www.usconcealedcarry.com/blog/in-which-states-can-you-concealed-carry-and-drink-alcohol/

Vinzant, C. X. (2015). *Lawyers, Guns, and Money: One Man's Battle with the Gun Industry.* St. Martin's Press.

Violence Policy Center. (2023). *Guns are the only consumer products in the United States not regulated by the federal government for health and safety.* Retrieved from Regulating the Gun Industr: https://vpc.org/regulating-the-gun-industry/

Waldman, M. (2015). *The Second Amendment: A Biography.* Simon & Schuster, Inc. .

Weapons of War. (2023). Retrieved from National Parks Service Museum Collection: https://www.nps.gov/museum/exhibits/revwar/guco/gucoweapons.html#:~:text=Muskets%20were%20smooth%2Dbored%2C%20single,was%20three%20shots%20per%20minute.

Weil DS, H. D. (1992, June 6). Loaded Guns in the Home: Analysis of a National Random Survey of Gun Owners. *JAMA, 267*(22), 3033–3037.

Winkler, A. (2011). *Gunfight: The Battle Over the Right to Bear Arms in America*. W. W. Norton & Company.

Wright, J. D. (2008). *Armed and Considered Dangerous 2nd Edition.* Routledge.

Yücel, D. O. (2019). Gun Addiction: A new addiction phenomenon. *Archives of Neuropsychiatry, 56*(3), 206-211.

Youngblood, E. (2022). *DEMENTIA AND FIREARM SAFETY.* Dimentia Education, Inc..

Zhao J, S. T. (2023, March 31). Association Between Daily Alcohol Intake and Risk of All-Cause Mortality: A Systematic Review and Meta-analyses. *JAMA Network Open, 6*(3).

Made in the USA
Middletown, DE
28 August 2023